Courage for the Crisis

Amid all the terrors of a disintegrating civilization some will stand unmoved. Drawing spiritual sustenance from the word of God, they will find ample courage for the crisis.

by *Arthur S. Maxwell*

Author of "This Mighty Hour," "Great Prophecies for Our Time," "Your Bible and You," "The Coming King," "The Bible Story," etc.

Courage for the Crisis

Strength for Today
Hope for Tomorrow

How to Find Peace of Mind and Fortitude of Spirit for the Dangerous Days Ahead

PACIFIC PRESS PUBLISHING ASSOCIATION
Mountain View, California

Preface

No one needs to be told that the world is moving into ever-deepening crisis. The tragic fact is obvious to all. Toynbee and Spengler, Niebuhr and Tillich, have been speaking of it for decades. Recently the pace of analysis has quickened. Scarcely a month passes without a book being published by some philosopher, historian, or theologian, dissecting current trends and warning of the imminent peril to civilization.

Thinking people are genuinely afraid of the future. They are convinced that mankind is moving toward some major tragedy. They may differ as to its nature, but not about its certainty. And the fear of it is causing depression, frustration, and despair to envelop the hearts of millions in a pall of gloom.

What we all need in this "time of troubles," as Toynbee calls it, is not merely knowledge of the crisis, but courage to meet it. We need to build up reserves of mental and spiritual fortitude sufficient to face any calamity victoriously. We need to develop an inner calm that will remain unruffled no matter what may happen. We must learn how to greet the future with a cheer and stand unmoved in the evil day.

Where shall peace of mind and tranquillity of spirit be found? The answer embraces the purpose and scope of this book. It is our conviction that there exist sources of spiritual strength which may be tapped by all who sense their need of it; and that from them flows courage sufficient for every emergency.

The headwaters are to be found in the heart of God, the eternal Spring of faith, hope, and love, but the healing streams course along diverse channels. Courage may flow into our hearts from the knowledge that God is Creator and Sustainer of the universe, or from evidence that He is the Lord of history, directing the course of nations as He works out His eternal purpose, or from the fulfillment of His predictions concerning men and peoples; or from the many Bible promises of His care and protection; or from the cross itself, with its dramatic assurance of God's concern for the human race; or from those essentials of Christian living such as Bible study, prayer, worship, and ministry to others.

Such are some of the sources of true courage—courage sufficient for every trial, courage that will endure undiminished until the worst is over and darkness yields to light, and night to day. This book presents anew their eternal potency. If perchance it should bring to the reader new strength for today and new hope for tomorrow, it will not have been written in vain.

Arthur S. Maxwell.

Acknowledgments
Unless otherwise indicated, Scripture references in this volume are quoted from the King James Version.

Quotations from the "New English Bible," copyrighted 1961, are reprinted by permission of The Delegates of the Oxford University Press and The Syndics of the Cambridge University Press; those from the "Revised Standard Version of the Bible," copyrighted 1946 and 1952, by permission of the Division of Christian Education, National Council of Churches; and those from Dr. Moffatt's "New Translation of the Bible," by permission of Hodder and Stoughton, Ltd.

Other quotations used by permission are from the article "Sanctuary—the Secret of a Peaceful Heart," by Margaret Blair Johnson, in "Guideposts," May 1953 (Guideposts Associated, Inc., Carmel, New York); from the book "Profiles in Courage," by John F. Kennedy (Harper and Brothers, New York); and the book "The American Sex Revolution," by Pitirim A. Sorokin (Porter Sargent Publisher, Boston, Massachusetts).

Contents

Some Will Be Brave

The crisis ahead will put us all to sterner tests than any previous generation endured. Many will break under the strain and go to pieces. But some will stand unmoved. They will not panic. They will not give way to despair.

Like ships securely anchored to the ocean floor they will ride out the wildest storms.

Like castles built solidly on granite crags they will withstand the worst assaults.

Like giant trees with roots deep bedded in the earth they will resist the fiercest hurricanes.

Drawing spiritual sustenance from hidden springs of faith they will find strength for today, hope for tomorrow, and courage sufficient for the crisis.

—See page 8.

Part One

THE GATHERING STORM

By their invention of rockets, satellites, hydrogen bombs, and a thousand other marvels, scientists have fashioned a sword of Damocles which now hangs precariously above us all.

KEN GUNALL, ARTIST   © P. P. P. A.

1

SWORD
OF DAMOCLES

*F*OR speaking indiscreetly
to King Dionysius of Syracuse during a royal banquet,
Damocles—who lived in the fourth century B.C.—was
condemned to sit beneath a naked sword suspended
by a single hair. Both Cicero and Horace tell the
story, and it has come down the ages as a striking
illustration of the imminence of deadly peril.

People are quoting the incident freely today. Not
in reference to one man, but to all men. In the opinion
of most thinking people, the whole human race is
now sitting in that chair, with total destruction hang-
ing by a hair above its head.

No ordinary peril threatens mankind today. The

sword above our heads is a calamity of fearful proportions without precedent in history. If and when it falls millions will die from nuclear explosions. Millions more will be doomed to lingering death from radiation, lethal chemicals, nerve gases, and disease germs. Great cities will be blasted into total ruin, the land will be sterilized, the water contaminated, the air corrupted.

"Not one but a thousand swords of Damocles dangle over us," said Jules Moch of France, addressing a recent international gathering.

How near is this disaster?

Nobody knows. But it may well be much closer than anyone dares to think.

Along the east coast of England, well hidden from prying eyes, are several strange instruments, each resembling the console of a giant organ. Beside each of them sit two highly trained officers, one from the United States Air Force, and the other from Britain's R.A.F. Each officer has a key to the instrument, one complementary to the other. Both men sit with earphones attached awaiting orders from Washington and London to insert the keys, adjust the instrument from peace to war, and release a salvo of hydrogen-headed missiles toward pinpointed targets a thousand miles away.

No provision has been made for reloading. There wouldn't be time. Within minutes an answering salvo would arrive, consuming men, machines, and unfired missiles in a fearful holocaust. Within hours World War III would be won or lost, leaving the earth a smoldering mass of radioactive ashes.

So near is total catastrophe.

Moving silently and swiftly under the oceans are the first nuclear-powered submarines, each armed with Polaris missiles, each missile loaded with a hydrogen warhead capable of destroying an entire metropolis. Cruising well within range of potential enemy targets, these ships of death stand ready to release their devastating weapons at a moment's notice. One word from the Pentagon would set their computers working, lift their rockets into firing position, and release them on their errands of destruction.

So close are we to that day of doom which men so long have feared.

In a windowless building in Colorado Springs stands a huge plastic map of North America on which is plotted the course of every moving object which passes the intricate radar screen constructed to warn of the approach of enemy planes, missiles, or submarines. Any object not immediately identified is subjected to instant investigation. Nothing is left to chance. With only seconds to spare for action, one mistake could be disastrous.

On October 5, 1960, radar signals reflected from the moon were momentarily misinterpreted as coming from approaching missiles, providing three businessmen with an experience of sickening terror.

The executives—Thomas Watson, president of International Business Machines; Charles H. Percy, president of Bell & Howell; and Peter G. Peterson, executive vice-president of Bell & Howell—were being shown the nation's defense headquarters.

"Our guide," Peterson said afterward, as reported in the San Francisco *Chronicle,* "showed us equipment designed to detect the presence of missiles. On a lighted panel was a series of numbers, running from 1 through 5.

"We were told if No. 1 flashed it meant only routine objects in the air. If No. 2 flashed, it meant there were a few more unidentified objects, but nothing suspicious.

"If No. 5 flashed," he continued, "it was highly probable that objects in the air were moving toward America. An attack was likely."

The three executives watched the screen, intent upon its operation. As they watched, the numbers changed from 1 to 2. Then a pause, and No. 3 appeared.

The numbers continued to move, reaching 4 and triggering the giant defense command into action. Key NORAD generals ran from their offices, converging on the room.

Then the number rose to 5.

Peterson and his friends were quickly escorted into another office. Stunned, they waited through twenty minutes of "absolute terror," until a NORAD officer entered the room and revealed the mistake.

So peril-conscious are the men who guard America!

Early in 1961 the U.S.S.R. put a seven-ton satellite into orbit, which in turn fired a rocket toward Venus, a spectacular scientific achievement demonstrating the feasibility of placing huge satellites in the sky loaded with hydrogen explosives to be dropped at will on preselected targets.

On December 28, 1960, Dr. Ralph E. Lapp told the American Association for the Advancement of Science that the United States now has a stockpile of atomic weapons equal to 50,000 A-bombs of the size that smashed Hiroshima. "Minuteman and Polaris missiles can carry 600-pound warheads with the explosive power of 500,000 tons of TNT. The B-52 bomber can carry two weapons with a total blast power of 45,000,000 tons of TNT. . . . The B-70 bomber could carry weapons with the power of 100,-000,000 tons."

Even more significant is the fact revealed by Sir Charles P. Snow to the same group of scientists that within six years a dozen nations will have atomic bombs, some of which, he said, will inevitably explode through "accident, folly, or madness."

So close are we to complete annihilation!

No wonder people are worried! No wonder they are losing heart! Gradually the awful truth is dawning on men's minds that, in the event of nuclear war, even those spared death by blast, fire, or radiation would find life scarcely worth living. The whole intricate fabric of civilization would be destroyed. Transportation, communication, and food distribution would come to a standstill. There would be no groceries in the supermarkets, no gas at the gas stations, no money in the banks. Stocks would be worthless. Law and order would be nonexistent. Houses left standing would be commandeered by refugees. Bandits would roam and rob at will. Chaos would reign everywhere.

Besides these terrors still others loom.

"Second among the specters that haunt mankind," says the editor of the *Bulletin of Atomic Scientists* (June, 1960) "is that of biological and chemical warfare." Long shrouded in official secrecy, this new peril is now receiving increasing publicity as its awful potency becomes more generally understood.

Disease-spreading, nerve-destroying bombs are capable of rendering whole armies impotent and causing millions of civilians to become incapable of resistance. Comparatively inexpensive, these weapons can be mass-produced by small nations as well as large, and without danger of detection.

"However difficult the international control of atomic weapons may be," says the *Bulletin* editor, "the international control of bacteriological and chemical weapons seems incomparably more difficult. . . . The means of dispersal of chemical and biological agents of warfare are . . . adapted to dispersal from planes and submarines, by conventional and rocket missiles, as well as by saboteurs."

Some of the newly developed chemicals are so potent that, to quote Norman Cousins, editor of the *Saturday Review* (July 23, 1960), "a liquid droplet the size of a pencil dot on the skin will penetrate surface tissue and kill a man within ten to fifteen minutes." A small, easily concealed container of disease germs tossed into a reservoir would be sufficient to paralyze a whole metropolis or start a nationwide epidemic.

This type of warfare, now far beyond the planning stage, could prove to be as deadly as nuclear war. Not only would combatants and noncombatants die by millions, but millions more in countries not immediately concerned in the conflict would be stricken. What remnants might be left of medical and nursing facilities and the Red Cross would be totally inadequate to meet the resultant colossal needs.

No wonder those who look into the future are appalled by what they see.

"No words are adequate to describe the magnitude or the consequences for mankind of the changes which have transpired during the past decade," said Roy G. Ross, General Secretary of the National Council of Churches, in his report to the Fifth General Assembly in San Francisco, December, 1960. "Writers and speakers have vied with each other in setting forth the drama of these changes. But no one of them has been able fully to register the emotions of man as he stands before the vast new knowledge which has been unfolded, the tremendous power which has been unleashed, and the even more awesome mysteries which still remain."

Lamenting "the turbulence of this revolutionary, nuclear-space age," and the fact that "our planet is tragically shadowed by conflicts and by threat of annihilation through thermonuclear war," a resolution passed at this same gathering declared that "the crisis of our time is not only, or even mainly, military and technological; the issues involve all dimensions of man's life; they are political, economic, cultural, and psychological; even more profoundly, they are moral and spiritual. . . . At issue in our world are questions of faith and unfaith: the meaning of life and history,

7

the nature and destiny of man, the values and purposes of human societies, the understanding of God and His will for the world."

The sword above our heads is all-inclusive in its menace. It dangles precariously above every nation, every family, every individual, on the face of the globe. It threatens everyone's home, family, possessions, and way of life.

Nor can anyone escape it by turning his head and wishing it were not there. It won't go away. The blade keeps on swinging. And the thread that holds it grows thinner and more frayed each passing day.

Inevitably, a crisis such as this, so terrifying, so universal, so altogether unprecedented, will put us all to sterner test than any previous generation endured. Some will break under the strain. Some will panic and go to pieces. Some will be crushed by disillusionment. Others will give way to wild, reckless abandon as they see their hopes and plans destroyed.

But some will stand unmoved. They will not panic. They will not go to pieces. They will not give way to despair.

Like ships securely anchored to the ocean floor they will ride out the wildest storms.

Like castles built solidly on granite crags they will withstand the worst assaults.

Like giant trees with roots deep bedded in the earth they will resist the fiercest hurricanes.

Drawing spiritual sustenance from hidden springs of faith they will find strength for today, hope for tomorrow, and courage sufficient for the crisis.

2

BROKEN CISTERNS

*I*N THE picturesque language of his time, the prophet Jeremiah, speaking for God, rebuked his people for building "broken cisterns."

"My people have committed two evils," he said; "they have forsaken Me the fountain of living waters, and hewed them out cisterns, broken cisterns, that can hold no water." Jeremiah 2:13.

An unfailing source of courage and hope was available to them, but they preferred to build their own. It seemed more reasonable to trust in plans which they themselves had devised; but their plans failed and the hopes they reposed in them drained away through cracks in these worthless cisterns.

All down the centuries men have been building faulty cisterns. In one long sequence of disappointments they have seen their best-laid schemes for peace and prosperity collapse and disintegrate.

Still fresh in many memories is the fate of the League of Nations. What high hopes centered in that organization! Millions believed it would provide a panacea for all earth's ills, a solution for all its problems. But despite its widely acclaimed inauguration it proved to be nought but a poor little makeshift cistern. All too soon its walls cracked and the hopes reposed in it seeped away.

Undaunted, men built again. They transferred the location from Switzerland to the United States. They changed the architecture from the gleaming white marble *Palais des Nations* on the shores of Lake Geneva to a steel-and-glass structure on Manhattan Island. They called it the United Nations, and as time went on draped a hundred flags in front of it. But within ten years of its inception it began to reveal similar signs of weakness. Today this "last best hope of man" —as many have called it—is generally recognized to be virtually helpless and bankrupt, another man-made cistern coming apart at the seams.

Disarmament conferences have turned out to be equally disappointing. I well recall the famous gathering held in Geneva, Switzerland, in 1931, thirteen years after the close of World War I. Delegates came from almost every nation. Impassioned oratory from the greatest statesmen of the time stirred new hope that the agelong search for a warless world was about to succeed. Hour after hour and day after day I listened to those earnest speeches, wondering if perchance some measure of progress might be made toward the goal.

There was none. Even while the delegates were still in session strife broke out between the Japanese and Chinese, precursor of World War II, eight years later.

Fifteen years after the close of that fearful conflict, delegates to yet another disarmament conference assembled once more in Geneva. Faces were different, but the purpose was the same. This time more dramatic suggestions were made, indicative of the increasingly urgent need for action.

Russia proposed total abolition of conventional troops within three years, elimination of foreign military bases, and destruction of nuclear weapons.

The West countered with a more gradual plan, including the creation of an International Disarmament Organization with powers of supervision and inspection of the various stages of disarmament as they might be carried out.

For months the arguments continued amid growing mistrust and rising tempers. At last the meeting broke up in failure. Like all those which had preceded it, this cistern also cracked, leaked, and dried up in hopeless frustration.

Summitry is another broken cistern. For a time some famous statesmen believed in it. "Get the leaders together," they urged, "and the worst problems will be quickly solved."

For ten years after Winston Churchill coined the phrase "meeting at the summit," more and more people planned and worked for such a gathering, confident that it would mark a significant forward step in international relations. Naïvely they pictured Eisenhower, Macmillan, De Gaulle, and Khrushchev closeted together in friendly fellowship, exchanging pleasantries, swapping jokes, perhaps even playing golf, as they worked out solutions to the world's problems.

As time passed these trickles of optimism swelled into a mighty stream which, piling up in this cistern, created a vast reservoir of hope that could have proved of inestimable blessing to mankind. Wisely exploited, it could have dissolved agelong enmities, abolished nuclear weapons, lifted the burden of armaments from all nations, given an unprecedented boost to world trade, and lifted the standard of living for countless millions the world around.

Two thousand newsmen from all countries converged on Paris to behold this dream come true and proclaim it in glowing words to all mankind. Anticipations were never brighter. A warless world was never nearer.

Alas, though the four leaders arrived, the muchheralded conference never convened. Suddenly, without warning, someone threw a switch and blasted this cistern to irretrievable ruin. Swiftly the pent-up waters of optimism ebbed away. By morning the reservoir of hope was empty. Only a sickening miasma of despair remained.

Likewise when the World Court was founded there

were some who cherished the belief that this organization might prove to be a notable advance toward the establishment of a law-abiding world community. They could not have been more mistaken. The Court has never functioned in any major dispute. Any hopes that reposed in this cistern have long since trickled away.

Similar hopes have rested—and still rest—in the World Council of Churches. Many earnest Christians believe that if all denominations would submerge their doctrinal differences and unite in one great religious organization speaking with one voice and purpose throughout the world, the kingdom of God would be at hand.

It might be so if everybody on earth were a truly converted Christian. But this being not only untrue but impossible of realization in the foreseeable future, the concept becomes yet another impractical dream, another leaky cistern in which people place their hopes in vain.

Thus mankind awaits the gathering storm, for the most part sustained by false hopes, trusting in worthless panaceas, and consequently doomed to bitter disillusionment.

Many, already sensing that there is no sure way to halt the onrushing calamity, are attempting to ignore it. They pose indifference, saying, "Let us eat, drink, and be merry, for tomorrow we die," or its more up-to-date rendering, "So what?" Their cisterns are in the form of bottles from which they draw temporary alcoholic stupefaction; cartons of cigarettes to "soothe" their overwrought nerves; or small cardboard boxes containing pills to "tranquilize" them or drugs to fan the flames of their fantasies.

The pity is that many people deliberately choose such poor, broken cisterns when, close at hand, in plain sight and easy reach, is a "fountain of living waters," a source of spiritual strength ample for every need.

This fountain never runs dry. Its waters are consistently refreshing and invigorating. They flow as strongly on the darkest days as when the sun is shining. They flow alike amid the gentle zephyrs of summer and winter's raging hurricanes. They will continue to flow through time's last and greatest storm.

Somehow we must find this fountain. For here and here alone we shall discover the strong faith, sure hope, and true courage we shall need for the crisis ahead.

3
WRITING
ON THE WALL

*T*WENTY-FIVE centuries ago, when the Babylonian Empire was at the height of its power, its capital became so wealthy that it was called the "golden city." Behind massive fortifications its citizens believed that no evil could ever befall them. They basked in a sense of security hitherto unknown by any community. So certain were they of the impregnability of their city that they felt free to indulge every sordid passion, reckless of the consequences.

Then it was that there appeared on the wall of King Belshazzar's palace those flaming words of condemnation: "God hath numbered thy kingdom, and finished it. . . . Thou art weighed in the balances, and art found wanting." Daniel 5:26, 27.

Nor was judgment long in coming. That very night, the Bible says, "was Belshazzar the king of the Chaldeans slain. And Darius the Median took the kingdom." Verses 30, 31.

Babylon need not have fallen. A previous king—Nebuchadnezzar—had been counseled by the prophet Daniel: "Break off thy sins by righteousness, and thine iniquities by showing mercy to the poor; if it may be a lengthening of thy tranquillity." Daniel 4:27.

Nebuchadnezzar heeded the warning, but his successors forgot it. Temporary reform was followed by worse iniquities, culminating in Belshazzar's feast, the writing on the wall—and doom.

This sequence of events, this decline from power through perversity to oblivion, is traceable through almost every nation and empire of history. This was the course of Medo-Persia, Greece, and Rome. Of Egypt, Tyre, and Carthage. Of the German Empire, the Austro-Hungarian Empire, and of Russia under the czars.

Invisibly but inexorably, a nation's sins are recorded. They pile up on the balances of heaven until finally the scales tilt and probation runs out. Then appears the writing on the wall, followed soon by judgment.

Today the whole world is involved. Modern Babylon encompasses the earth. Never was there so much prosperity. Never were protecting ramparts so high. Stone walls and bronze gates have become nuclear bombs and rockets. But as in every ancient empire, behind the "great deterrent" character disintegrates and lawlessness grows worse from year to year.

Addressing a symposium on nuclear education in New York recently, Dr. Charles W. Shilling of the Atomic Energy Commission declared: "We have been living aimless lives with disjointed purposes. Too many of us have been concerned with bigger incomes, bigger television screens, and bigger cars, and not with bigger ideas on how to live together on this globe, or with developing a backlog of scientific information on which our freedom and our very lives may soon depend."

He concluded his remarks by saying: "There is a justifiable uneasiness existing in America today related to our failure to live up to our moral capacity as a nation.

Still fresh in everybody's mind are the Congressional investigations into various phases of American life. Inquiry into the racketeering in labor unions produced an alarming report, including intimidation, intolerance, and embezzlement—all so foreign to the ideals and principles of the founding fathers.

Shortly thereafter came the investigation of TV quiz programs, revealing a sordid mass of trickery, falsehood, and fraud.

Then the spotlight turned upon radio music, and in particular upon the disk jockeys who, to a larger extent than anyone suspected, control it. Again, as platter after platter was turned over, a putrid stench emerged. A nasty new word was added to the nation's vocabulary—"payola," a synonym for the new type of graft that greed has spawned. About this same time *Look* magazine sent twelve reporters to discover the effect of these investigations upon the general public. Upon their return they declared that the TV and disk jockey scandals, the Sherman Adams and Van Doren cases, the conspiracies by union officials and Chicago policemen, were only incidents of an "epidemic of immorality." "On a national scale," they reported, "few seem immune to the cancer of moral indifference."

"A moral relativeness seems to have replaced the moral certitudes of the past," they commented. People feel it is all right to flout laws of which they disapprove, whether liquor, gambling, traffic, tax, or other types of laws. An insurance adjuster told them, "I hate to say this, but 75 per cent of the people we deal with now have no morals at all."

Quarter by quarter John Edgar Hoover issues his crime reports. The trend is always in the same direction. More murders, more assaults, more rapes, more burglaries, more thefts, more vandalism, more juvenile delinquency—a sad and terrifying picture.

Every day newspapers are filled with stories of savage, brutal attacks on innocent people. Bank robberies occur with such frequency that they have become an item of secondary interest.

Equally sinister is the universal school of crime conducted by the TV industry, by which millions of children and youth are fed a daily diet of horror and sadism, shooting and killing.

The dissemination of pornographic publications, now a multimillion-dollar industry, is another growing evil, supported by large numbers of people who have lost all sense of moral standards. Modern novels, movies, and movie advertisments betray the same ugly trend. So do the tragic divorce statistics and the appalling number of illegitimate births.

In his book entitled *The American Sex Revolution,* Professor P. A. Sorokin, of Harvard University, says: "Our civilization has become so preoccupied with sex that it now oozes from all pores of American life." "We are completely surrounded by the rising tide of sex, which is flooding every compartment of our culture, every section of our social life."—Pages 19, 54.

In the opinion of this distinguished authority in social science, this trend, unless arrested, could well destroy Western civilization as it once destroyed both Greece and Rome.

"The people of America are richer than any nation in history," says Dr. Roy G. Ross, General Secretary of the National Council of Churches. "We have equipped ourselves with a great array of gadgets and devices for comfortable living. We are nearer to the elimination of poverty than the most optimistic dared hope fifty years ago. We have made great advances in the elimination of the diseases afflicting humanity. We have extended the span of life and provided increasing protection for our infants, our older citizens and the disabled. We have increased our leisure time and our capacity for travel. . . . But notwithstanding these facts, Christian people are aware that something is wrong and they are restless."—*Report to the Fifth General Assembly,* page 13.

Among America's deficiencies, Dr. Ross lists the following: First, lack of any great spiritual purpose; second, lack of clear concepts of morals and standards of conduct; third, lack of concern for underprivileged segments of the population; fourth, weakening of the family unit and a loosening conviction regarding the sanctity of love; fifth, the rising tide of juvenile delinquency.

"Until a larger portion of our people can again arrive at a real as compared with a nominal belief in a God-controlled universe where some absolutes in moral and ethical principles obtain," he says; "until more adults believe in these principles to the point of making them the guide to their own conduct, and of demanding that they shall guide the conduct of government, business operations, and social procedure; until a larger number of parents regain their belief in the home as an institution for developing sound character patterns; until we can give our youth some sense of purpose beyond material advance; our nation will fall short of her potential inner strength for influencing future world trends, and we are bound to be an uneasy and conscience-stricken people."—*Ibid.,* p. 17.

Grave indeed is America's peril today. Not only because of the corrupting effects of evil and the weakness accruing from the gradual disappearance of moral purpose, but even more because the record of all this decadence and failure is piling up fast in the balances of heaven. True, there is much good on one side of the scales, but what of the other? What of all the crime, vandalism, pornography, divorce, alcoholism, gambling, self-indulgence, and greed recorded there?

If history has one lesson above all others for this country and the world today, it is that national apostasy brings national disaster. "God is not mocked: for whatsoever a man soweth, that shall he also reap." Galatians 6:7.

All down the centuries, empires, nations, and cities have been weighed in the balances and found wanting. They have seen the writing on the wall and learned, too late, of approaching doom.

To ancient Nineveh, the rich, arrogant, corrupt capital of Assyria, God sent this warning: "Woe to the bloody city, all full of lies. . . . I am against you. . . . I will . . . treat you with contempt, and make you a gazingstock. And all who look on you will shrink from you and say, Wasted is Nineveh; who will bemoan her?" Nahum 3:1-7, R.S.V.

Shortly thereafter Assyria was overthrown, never to rise again.

When the highly privileged kingdom of Judah gravely disappointed its divine Founder, the prophet Jeremiah brought to it a dramatic message. Breaking an earthen bottle before its rulers, he said, "Thus saith the Lord of hosts; Even so will I break this people and this city, as one breaketh a potter's vessel, that cannot be made whole again." Jeremiah 19:11.

Months later invaders from Babylon brought destruction and captivity to a people who thought such things could never happen to them.

Addressing Jerusalem with tears in His voice, Jesus Christ foretold the doom of the city which had lost its way and failed its destiny: "O Jerusalem, Jerusalem, thou that killest the prophets, and stonest them which are sent unto thee, how often would I have gathered thy children together, even as a hen gathereth her chickens under her wings, and ye would not! Behold, your house is left unto you desolate." Matthew 23:37, 38.

Within forty years Roman armies sacked the city, leaving "not one stone upon another."

Today similar words of warning echo from nation to nation around the world. Upon the walls of every palace and parliament, every congress and hall of justice, every military base and college campus, every office and factory, every theater, movie house, and race track, a hand from heaven is writing the awesome, fateful words, "Weighed in the balances and found wanting!"

This is the third dimension of the gathering storm. The tragic events soon to burst upon the world will not be merely the result of man's tampering with natural forces beyond his capacity to tame. They will not be just the inevitable aftermath of foolish planning and misplaced hopes. They will also be a judgment. They will have a moral aspect and bear the hallmark of divine retribution.

And it is this that magnifies the present crisis above any hitherto experienced. Involved are not only man's temporal possessions and way of life, but also his eternal destiny. Ahead, in the deepening darkness, there is not only calamity on a stupendous scale, but confrontation with the One whose laws have been flouted, whose love has been spurned, whose honor has been trampled in the dust.

For this encounter the greatest courage of all will be required, a courage of purer essence than any that war or natural disaster demands.

Needed also will be courage to resist evil with holy boldness, to endure persecution without flinching, to stand for right though the heavens fall.

Where shall such spiritual fortitude as this be found?

Where indeed?

Perchance in the pages that follow.

Part Two

COURAGE
FROM
GOD

Amid life's worst storms it is comforting to know that there is a hand on the helm. It is the hand of God who, with infinite wisdom and understanding, will bring His people safely through them all.

HARRY ANDERSON, ARTIST   © R. & H.

4

HAND
ON THE HELM

SOME years ago I was
crossing the Atlantic on the "Queen Mary" when she
ran into a heavy storm. In the worst moments she
rolled so far over that I wondered if she would ever
right herself again. Simultaneously her bow rose and
fell with prodigious leaps, while every few minutes a
giant wave crashed against her side, causing the whole
fabric of the ship to shudder.

Like most of the other passengers, I lay on my bunk
seasick and helpless, yearning for land as a blind man
longs for sight. Had the fate of that great Cunarder
rested in my poor hands during that night of anguish,
she would surely have foundered. Fortunately for all

aboard, it didn't. Instead, there was a captain on the bridge made of sterner stuff than I, a man who had spent his life on the ocean, a man of experience, wisdom, and good judgment. In him we all trusted and he brought us safely to port.

Any courage I had on that voyage—and sometimes, I confess, mine was at a very low ebb—came from confidence in the man whose hand was on the helm. Far below—on D-deck, to be precise—I could neither see nor hear him, but it was enough to know that he was there, in charge.

So in the gathering storm now threatening all mankind. To endure and outlast it we shall need to trust someone far wiser and stronger than ourselves. Attempting to battle it alone will invite both disillusionment and despair.

But whom can we trust? Certainly none of the political figures whose names crash the headlines from week to week. They come and go with no semblance of permanence or any indication of special wisdom.

Not many years ago some people thought Benito Mussolini had all the answers. He hadn't. He was a dismal failure. So, too, was Adolf Hitler, though for a decade he rode a high tide of popularity among his people. Roosevelt, Churchill, Stalin, Eisenhower, all great figures in their day, are now but names in history books for a new generation to memorize.

Religious leaders are equally transitory. In most Protestant churches they don't last as long as Congressmen. Even the pope, usually elected in old age, has but a brief life expectancy.

Wise indeed is the counsel of the psalmist: "Put not your trust in princes, nor in the son of man, in whom there is no help. His breath goeth forth, he returneth to his earth; in that very day his thoughts perish." Psalm 146:3, 4.

Perhaps great preachers like Peale or McCracken of New York, or great evangelists like Billy Graham, could provide the moral and spiritual leadership required? They couldn't. And they would be the first to reject the suggestion. "Don't trust us," they would say, "trust God!"

And that is exactly what we must somehow learn to do. For only God is worthy of our complete and abiding confidence in this critical hour. Only He is great enough to handle all the tumultuous forces involved; good enough to be both absolutely just and infinitely kind to all; and wise enough to understand the human problem in all its vast complexity and bring about its final solution.

Echoing down the corridors of time from another period of storm and tragedy comes this meaningful entreaty: "Be still, and know that I am God." Psalm 46:10.

"Though the earth be removed, and though the mountains be carried into the midst of the sea; though the waters thereof roar and be troubled, though the mountains shake with the swelling thereof," we are to "be still, and know"—God. Verses 2, 3.

"When disaster strikes on British navy vessels," says Margaret Blair Johnson in "Sanctuary—The Secret of a Peaceful Heart," " 'The Still' is instantly blown. It means: 'Prepare to do the wise thing.' When the signal is piped, few men know the wise thing. But in the moments of calm enforced by that signal they find it. Each man calculates his position and checks his resources. By observing 'The Still,' they rout confusion and frequently avert catastrophe.

"So with our personal emergencies. Few of us instantly know the wise thing. 'If only I could *know* what to do!' we cry, forgetting that the order of procedure is: *Be still!*

"No matter how little you *know*, or even how little you think you have faith to believe, the next time you need sanctuary stop instantly all feverish activity and do what those who have found sanctuary do: '*Be still* and know. . . .'

"Countless hard-pressed men and women find in religion their 'place of certain shelter' when their hearts cry for spiritual sanctuary. We are again laying hold on the central reality that all religion offers: 'God is our refuge and strength, a very present help in trouble.'"—*Guideposts,* May, 1953.

But how can we know God if we cannot see Him? How can we be sure He is on the bridge, with His hand on the helm, when we are, as it were, far below in the bowels of the ship?

By faith. That is, by believing what He has told us about Himself.

Where may this be found? In the Bible, which above all else is a revelation of God, lovingly provided by Him, that you and I might know Him, understand Him, trust Him, love Him, and draw from Him those spiritual resources needed to meet life's crises with fortitude.

Read what the Bible says about God.

First, God is a living person. He is not a myth, a figment of the imagination. Rather, "He is the living God, and steadfast forever." Daniel 6:26. "He is the living God and the everlasting King." Jeremiah 10: 10, R.S.V.

He has a dwelling place: "Hear Thou in heaven Thy dwelling place." 1 Kings 8:39.

He can see and hear: "The eyes of the Lord are over the righteous, and His ears are open unto their prayers." 1 Peter 3:12.

He thinks and remembers: "For He knoweth our frame; He remembereth that we are dust." Psalm 103:14.

He is generous: "No good thing will He withhold from them that walk uprightly." Psalm 84:11.

He is eager to be helpful: "I am the Lord thy God which teacheth thee to profit, which leadeth thee by the way that thou shouldest go." Isaiah 48:17.

Second, God is eternal. He endures. He is not here today and gone tomorrow. He is "the same yesterday, and today, and forever." Hebrews 13:8.

There never was a time when He did not exist: "Before the mountains were brought forth, or ever Thou hadst formed the earth and the world, even from everlasting to everlasting, Thou art God." Psalm 90:2.

There never will be a time when He will cease to exist: "For I lift up My hand to heaven, and say, I live forever." Deuteronomy 32:40.

His kingdom is everlasting: "Thy kingdom is an everlasting kingdom, and Thy dominion endureth throughout all generations." Psalm 145:13.

He is immortal: "Now unto the King eternal, immortal, invisible, the only wise God, be honor and glory forever and ever." 1 Timothy 1:17.

Third, God is omnipotent. He has all power at His command: "Both riches and honor come of Thee, and Thou reignest over all; and in Thine hand is power and might; and in Thine hand it is to make great, and to give strength unto all." 1 Chronicles 29:12.

There is nothing He cannot do: "I know that Thou canst do everything, and that no thought can be withholden from Thee." Job 42:2.

He is free of all restraint: "Our God is in the heavens: He hath done whatsoever He hath pleased." Psalm 115:3.

He considers nothing impossible. Said Jesus, "With God all things are possible." Matthew 19:26. "The Lord God omnipotent reigneth." Revelation 19:6.

Fourth, God is omniscient. He knows everything. There is nothing hidden from Him: "For His eyes are upon the ways of man, and He seeth all his goings." Job 34:21.

There is nothing He does not understand: "His understanding is infinite." Psalm 147:5.

There is no word that He does not hear: "For there is not a word in my tongue, but, lo, O Lord, Thou knowest it altogether." Psalm 139:4.

There is nothing He does not see. Wrote David: "Whither shall I go from Thy Spirit? or whither shall

I flee from Thy presence? If I ascend up into heaven, Thou art there: if I make my bed in hell, behold, Thou art there. If I take the wings of the morning, and dwell in the uttermost parts of the sea; even there shall Thy hand lead me, and Thy right hand shall hold me." Psalm 139:7-10.

Darkness makes no difference to Him: "Yea, the darkness hideth not from Thee; but the night shineth as the day: the darkness and the light are both alike to Thee." Verse 12.

He is the source and wellspring of all knowledge and wisdom: "O the depth of the riches both of the wisdom and knowledge of God! how unsearchable are His judgments, and His ways past finding out!" Romans 11:33.

Fifth, God is infinite. He is without limitations of any kind. Not only in power, wisdom, and knowledge, but also in righteousness: "My righteousness shall be forever, and My salvation from generation to generation." Isaiah 51:8.

In every thought, word, and deed He is altogether holy: "The Lord is righteous in all His ways, and holy in all His works." Psalm 145:17.

His infinite realm is ruled eternally in perfect rectitude: "Righteousness and judgment are the habitation of His throne." Psalm 97:2.

His mercy is likewise limitless: "The mercy of the Lord is from everlasting to everlasting upon them that fear Him." Psalm 103:17.

Such is the God the Bible reveals. He is infinitely powerful yet infinitely compassionate, infinitely wise yet infinitely good, infinitely just yet infinitely merciful.

And such is the One who says to us all as the gathering storm envelops us, "Be still, and know that I am God."

His is the hand on history's helm today—and on the helm of your life and mine.

Knowing Him, trusting Him, we shall find the courage we shall need to meet the coming crisis victoriously.

5

VIEW OF
THE THRONE

*F*ROM the far reaches of history comes a story of special helpfulness in these dark and dangerous days.

"In the year that King Uzziah died," writes the prophet Isaiah, "I saw also the Lord sitting upon a throne, high and lifted up, and His train filled the temple." Isaiah 6:1.

That must have been about 740 B.C. Uzziah's fifty-two-year reign over the kingdom of Judah had just ended and Isaiah's long ministry had just begun.

The times were much like our own. Military preparedness and the big deterrent were uppermost in men's minds. Fearing the Assyrians, the Egyptians, and the Philistines, King Uzziah had "strengthened himself exceedingly." He had built "towers in Jerusalem" and "towers in the desert," and had assembled a well-organized army of some 300,000 men that "went out to war by bands" and "made war with mighty power." Weapons had been provided in abundance, including "shields, and spears, and helmets, and habergeons, and bows, and slings to cast stones." Nor were they behind in novel methods of warfare, for "engines, invented by cunning men" were set up on the towers and bulwarks "to shoot arrows and great stones withal." 2 Chronicles 26:8-15.

But then, as now, false confidence in armaments was accompanied by moral decay. Isaiah's first message was a rebuke of apostasy. "Ah sinful nation," he said, "a people laden with iniquity, a seed of evildoers, children that are corrupters: they have forsaken the Lord, they have provoked the Holy One of Israel unto anger, they are gone away backward. . . . From the sole of the foot even unto the head there is no soundness in it; but wounds, and bruises, and putrefying sores." Isaiah 1:4-6.

Looming on the horizon was the shrewd and powerful Tiglath-pileser III, one of the great kings of Assyria. Ascending his throne in 745 B.C., he set out on a series of forays which in five years made him master of much of western Asia. It was then, in the fifth year of his reign, when his conquests were at flood tide, that King Uzziah died.

The concern throughout Judah can be imagined. What would be its fate now that its strong and trusted leader had passed away? Would Tiglath-pileser take this opportunity to move south and wipe out the little nation? Were the Assyrians about to overrun and dominate the whole world?

At this moment of profound anxiety and alarm Isaiah saw the Lord "sitting upon a throne, high and lifted up" while seraphim cried one to another, "Holy, holy, holy, is the Lord of hosts."

It was indeed a comforting vision. Judah's throne might be vacant, but God's was not. He was still there. And always would be there, world without end. Unchanged and unchanging through unending years, He would reign serenely over His universe forever and ever, "from everlasting to everlasting."

On earth there might be fear, uncertainty, and all the wild fever of self-preservation, but not in heaven. There, amid indescribable calm and peace beyond compare, there was time to sing of holiness.

On earth sin might reign and apostasy flourish, but not in the presence of God. There righteousness and goodness were pre-eminent, and would be always.

Earthly thrones might totter, kingdoms rise and fall, but the throne of God, sure-based on truth and virtue, would endure through all generations. From thence, unmoved by human turmoil or clamor, God would direct the affairs of nations with justice and judgment until His eternal purpose should be achieved.

If Isaiah had lacked courage up to this moment, his need was now supplied. Fortified by this vision of the throne of God, he faced the issues of his day with confidence, saying, "Here am I; send me." Isaiah 6:8.

In a time of grave perplexity Moses was given a similar vision (Exodus 24:10), as also was the prophet Micaiah (1 Kings 22:19), and Amos the dedicated herdsman (Amos 9:1). Years later, during the Babylonian captivity, both Daniel (Daniel 7:9) and Ezekiel (Ezekiel 1:1; 10:1-5) saw visions of the Lord upon His throne, as also did John on the Isle of Patmos during the persecution of the early church. Revelation 4:1-6.

These records suggest that in times of special need, when trials and perils abound, a glimpse of God upon His throne is sufficient to banish fear and restore both hope and courage to the heart.

You and I may not witness the same dazzling scenes of glory that the prophets of old beheld, but just turning our thoughts heavenward can accomplish the same result.

"Lift up your eyes!" is a frequent Biblical exhortation and is excellent counsel today. We need to look up from the events and conditions that trouble us and tell ourselves that God not only knows about them but is more concerned than we could possibly be. The very thought that He is in control, leading and directing according to His infinite wisdom, will give us equanimity of spirit and renew our courage.

In the midst of his long reign, Nebuchadnezzar was given seven years' punishment for pride and vainglory. At its conclusion he declared: "At the end of the days I, Nebuchadnezzar, lifted my eyes to heaven, and my reason returned to me, and I blessed the Most High, and praised and honored Him who lives forever; for

His dominion is an everlasting dominion, and His kingdom endures from generation to generation; all the inhabitants of the earth are accounted as nothing; and He does according to His will in the host of heaven and among the inhabitants of the earth; and none can stay His hand or say to Him, 'What doest Thou?'" Daniel 4:34, 35, R.S.V.

This heathen monarch did not see God as did the prophets of Israel, but lifting his eyes heavenward brought him healing and new hope. His reason returned to him. His judgment was no longer impaired. He saw everything in a new light. Humbly recognizing God's sovereignty over men and nations, he cried, "Now I, Nebuchadnezzar, praise and extol and honor the King of heaven; for all His works are right and His ways are just; and those who walk in pride He is able to abase." Verse 37, R.S.V.

As a result he returned to his royal duties renewed in body and soul, and "still more greatness was added" to him.

Daniel in the lions' den was granted no special vision of God, but evidence is plentiful that this good man took his eyes off the lions and turned them heavenward. In so doing he found the help he so desperately needed. Next morning, when King Darius came to the den to inquire concerning his safety, the prophet replied, "My God sent His angel and shut the lions' mouths, and they have not hurt me." Daniel 6:22, R.S.V.

Then it was that the king "wrote to all the peoples, nations, and languages that dwell in all the earth:

'Peace be multiplied to you. I make a decree, that in all my royal dominion men tremble and fear before the God of Daniel, for He is the living God, enduring forever; His kingdom shall never be destroyed, and His dominion shall be to the end. He delivers and rescues, He works signs and wonders in heaven and on earth, He who has saved Daniel from the power of the lions.' " Verses 25-28, R.S.V.

There is a mighty blessing in the upward look. Just thinking about God in a moment of crisis can mean all the difference between cringing fear and holy boldness. For He is the fountain of courage, the never-failing source of Christian fortitude.

No one knew this better than that stalwart Christian leader, the apostle Paul. On his last visit to Jerusalem, though warned again and again of "bonds and afflictions" awaiting him, he refused to be intimidated. "None of these things move me," he said, "neither count I my life dear unto myself, so that I might finish my course with joy, and the ministry, which I have received of the Lord Jesus, to testify the gospel of the grace of God." Acts 20:24.

The upward look sustained him. His worst trials he adjudged of little account as he let his mind dwell upon the Lord he loved, seated "on the right hand of the Majesty on high." Hebrews 1:3. Utterly convinced that the King of the universe was his friend, he feared nothing and nobody.

He had troubles innumerable—enough to crush the spirit of the bravest. Think what he suffered:

"Of the Jews five times received I forty stripes save

Convinced that God was his Friend, the apostle Paul was undisturbed by the storm that was battering his ship to pieces. To terror-stricken fellow passengers he cried, "Keep up your courage!"

one," he told the church at Corinth. "Thrice was I beaten with rods, once was I stoned, thrice I suffered shipwreck, a night and a day I have been in the deep; in journeyings often, in perils of waters, in perils of robbers, in perils by mine own countrymen, in perils by the heathen, in perils in the city, in perils in the wilderness, in perils in the sea, in perils among false brethren; in weariness and painfulness, in watchings often, in hunger and thirst, in fastings often, in cold and nakedness. Beside those things that are without, that which cometh upon me daily, the care of all the churches." 2 Corinthians 11:24-28.

Did all this bring him to despair? No indeed.

With amazing spiritual buoyancy he wrote: "We are troubled on every side, yet not distressed; we are perplexed, but not in despair; persecuted, but not forsaken; cast down, but not destroyed." "For which cause we faint not; but though our outward man perish, yet the inward man is renewed day by day. For our light affliction, which is but for a moment, worketh for us a far more exceeding and eternal weight of glory; while we look not at the things which are seen, but at the things which are not seen: for the things which are seen are temporal; but the things which are not seen are eternal." 2 Corinthians 4:8, 9, 16-18.

The New English Bible renders verses 16-18 thus: "No wonder we do not lose heart! Though our outward humanity is in decay, yet day by day we are inwardly renewed. Our troubles are slight and short-lived; and their outcome an eternal glory which outweighs them far. Meanwhile our eyes are fixed, not on the things that are seen, but on the things that are unseen: for what is seen passes away; what is unseen is eternal."

Here Paul revealed the secret of his indomitable spirit. By faith he looked beyond the troubles that surrounded him and fastened his gaze upon the throne of God, finding there an inexhaustible reservoir of strength and courage. No wonder he did not lose heart!

Perhaps the most striking example of his fortitude under stress occurred during his last voyage across the Mediterranean as a prisoner of the Romans. Not far from Crete the ship, with 276 persons aboard, ran into a heavy storm. For several days and nights the tempest raged, battering the vessel so severely that both crew and passengers lost all hope of seeing land again.

Then, as the ship pitched and rolled amid the giant combers, this man of God somehow made his way to where most of the terrified crew and seasick passengers were gathered and brought them this heartening message:

"I urge you not to lose heart; not a single life will be lost, only the ship. For last night there stood by me an angel of the God whose I am and whom I worship. 'Do not be afraid, Paul,' he said; 'it is ordained that you shall appear before the Emperor; and, be assured, God has granted you the lives of all who are sailing with you.' So keep up your courage: I trust in God that it will turn out as I have been told." Acts 27:22-25, N.E.B.

And that is how it did turn out. His courage and God's providence carried the whole ship's company to safety on the island of Malta.

He saw no glowing vision of the throne of God as did Isaiah or Ezekiel in years long past, but he believed with all his heart that God was in complete control of the situation—just as you and I can believe today. "We walk by faith, not by sight," he said (2 Corinthians 5:7), or, as the New English Bible renders this passage: "Faith is our guide, we do not see Him."

That wonderful faith made God so real to Paul that with holy boldness he approached the throne of grace to "obtain mercy, and find grace to help in time of need." Hebrews 4:16. Thus when on that stormy night an angel flew from heaven to his aid, and located him in the dark, creaking, stench-filled hold of that sinking vessel, he was not surprised. It seemed exactly the right thing to happen. He had asked for help and his Friend the King of heaven sent it. What else would a true friend do?

Thus no trials or hardships depressed him. No disappointments or upset plans caused him to despair. Events that brought terror to others found him in perfect peace, radiating confidence and cheer.

We need courage like this today. We shall need it more tomorrow when the gathering storm breaks upon us in all its fury. And we can find it as Paul found it—and Isaiah and Moses and a host of others—by lifting up our eyes to see the Lord "sitting upon a throne, high and lifted up."

6

EYE ON THE FUTURE

O F ALL God's marvelous attributes none begets more confidence and courage than His ability to read the future. In times of perplexity it is wonderfully comforting to know that He is fully aware how everything is going to turn out. It is like traveling in a foreign country with a guide who was born there and knows everything about it.

Last time I went to Europe the travel agency assured me that it would be a "personally conducted" tour. Not that a representative would accompany me all the way, but in every place where I might need help some competent person would be available.

As things turned out it became almost uncanny the

way the well-trained personnel kept turning up to offer their services. In every important city someone knew exactly when and where I would arrive. Invariably, without fail, as my train stopped at the station a man would be standing on the platform—right outside my window!—ready to greet me by name, escort me to my hotel, discuss the next stage of my trip, and explain everything I needed to know in language I could understand.

This remarkably efficient service was, of course, due to the fact that the enterprising agency had sent full particulars of my itinerary ahead, thus giving me a delightful impression of their seeming omniscience.

In like manner, but with infinitely fuller knowledge, God is aware of all our plans and undertakings. He knows where we will be at any hour of the day or night —tomorrow, next week, or next year. He knows everything that is going to happen to us right down to the last day of our earthly pilgrimage.

He has an eye on the future. He knows the news before the newsmen. He knows what the outcome will be in Berlin, East Germany, Cuba, Thailand, Guatemala, or any other troubled land. He knows what Russia, France, Great Britain, or the United States will be doing a decade from now. The top-secret plans of the Kremlin and the Pentagon are open books to Him. Nothing that happens anywhere on earth takes Him by surprise.

How God is able to see events before they happen is one of the sublime mysteries of divinity. Someday, perhaps, He will explain it to us. In the meantime we need have no doubt that He possesses this remarkable power. Here is His own bold claim:

"I am God, and there is none like Me, declaring the end from the beginning, and from ancient times the things that are not yet done, saying, My counsel shall stand." Isaiah 46:9, 10.

Again: "Behold, the former things are come to pass, and new things do I declare: before they spring forth I tell you of them." Isaiah 42:9.

These are not vain boasts, but statements of fact. The evidence is clear that God can see "the end from the beginning" and tell things "before they spring forth."

History affords instance after instance of the exact fulfillment of predictions He has made through His prophets.

Early in the eighth century B.C., when the empire of Assyria was at the height of its power, Nahum predicted that its capital city Nineveh would become a total desolation, "empty, and void, and waste." Nahum 2:10. "With an overrunning flood He will make an utter end of the place." Nahum 1:8. Those were strong words and must have seemed absurd at the time. Probably some of Nahum's acquaintances dismissed them as wishful thinking or the rantings of a religious fanatic. It was as if some modern preacher should announce that Moscow, Paris, or Washington would soon be wiped off the face of the earth. And Nahum spoke long before hydrogen bombs, when the most potent weapons were slings and bows.

As years passed and Nineveh continued to prosper, some people no doubt taunted the prophet with having guessed wrong. But instead of retracting, he came back with this choice description of the city's fate: "All your fortresses are like fig trees with first-ripe figs—if shaken they fall into the mouth of the eater." Nahum 3:12, R.S.V.

While those about him lived in dread of the seemingly invincible Assyrian armies, Nahum remained calm and untroubled, certain of their ultimate defeat. His eye was on the future, as God had revealed it to him, and he was sure the revelation was true.

As, of course, it was. Within a hundred years Nineveh was overthrown by the Babylonians and thereafter gradually faded from history.

In the seventh century A.D. a battle was fought between the Romans and the Persians on the site where the Assyrian capital once stood. Describing the scene, the historian Gibbon wrote: "Eastward of the Tigris, at the end of the bridge of Mosul, the great Nineveh had formerly been erected: the city, and *even the ruins of the city, had long since disappeared;* the vacant space afforded a spacious field for the operations of the two armies."—Edward Gibbon, *The History of the Decline and Fall of the Roman Empire,* ch. 46, par. 24. (Italics supplied.)

"Even the ruins" had disappeared. Nineveh had indeed become "empty, and void, and waste." God, who reads the future, had described it perfectly!

Babylon's fate was foretold with similar accuracy. In the heyday of its power, while it was still known as the marvel of nations, two Hebrew prophets had the audacity to announce its complete destruction.

Isaiah, speaking as the mouthpiece of God, declared: "Babylon, the glory of kingdoms, the beauty of the Chaldees' excellency, shall be as when God overthrew Sodom and Gomorrah. It shall *never be inhabited,* neither shall it be dwelt in from generation to generation: neither shall the Arabian pitch tent there; neither shall the shepherds make their fold there. But wild beasts of the desert shall lie there; . . . and owls shall dwell there. . . . And her time is near to come." Isaiah 13:19-22.

The prophet Jeremiah added this equally dramatic prediction: "Declare ye among the nations; . . . Babylon is taken." "How is the hammer of the whole earth cut asunder and broken! how is Babylon become a desolation among the nations!" "It shall be *no more inhabited* forever; neither shall it be dwelt in from generation to generation." Jeremiah 50:2, 23, 39.

"And Babylon shall become heaps, a dwelling place for dragons, an astonishment, and an hissing, *without an inhabitant.*" Jeremiah 51:37.

Notice how both prophets mentioned that the city should become deserted, "without an inhabitant." This was being dangerously specific and some of their friends may well have said to them, "Don't you think you are going a little too far? After all, Babylon is the biggest city man has ever built."

But the prophets did not change their prediction. They knew it had come to them from One who knows the future as well as the past, and that time would prove it true.

It did. As noted in a previous chapter, judgment,

swift and terrible, came upon Babylon on the night of Belshazzar's famous feast. Thereafter, as century succeeded century, the once mighty city gradually crumbled away, its walls, palaces, and temples slowly fading from sight beneath the sands of the encroaching desert. For generations it was a lost city, with no one even knowing where it once had stood.

In 1845, and again 1850, the famous archaeologist Layard explored the site, afterward describing it as follows:

"Shapeless heaps of rubbish cover for many an acre the face of the land. . . . On all sides, fragments of glass, marble, pottery, and inscribed brick are mingled with that peculiar nitrous and blanched soil, which, bred from the remains of ancient habitations, checks or destroys vegetation, and renders the site of Babylon a naked and hideous waste. Owls start from the scanty thickets, and the foul jackal skulks through the furrows."—Austen H. Layard, *Discoveries in the Ruins of Nineveh and Babylon* (1853), page 484.

In recent years excavations have continued in this area and many remarkable finds have been made; but the ancient city remains a desolate, roofless tomb, "without an inhabitant."

With what amazing precision did God foretell the future in this case!

He had something to say, too, about Egypt. About the year 587 B.C., while the land of the Pharaohs was still a power in the earth, the prophet Ezekiel was directed to say: "The word of the Lord came unto me, saying, Son of man, set thy face against Pharaoh king of Egypt, and prophesy against him, and against all Egypt: speak, and say, Thus saith the Lord God; Behold, I am against thee, Pharaoh king of Egypt, the great dragon that lieth in the midst of his rivers, which hath said, My river is mine own, and I have made it for myself." Ezekiel 29:1-3.

Then the prophet uttered this astounding prediction concerning Egypt's future: "It shall be the basest of the kingdoms; neither shall it exalt itself any more above the nations: for I will diminish them, that they shall no more rule over the nations." Verse 15.

More than twenty-five centuries have passed since then. At any moment during this long period some powerful leader might have arisen to restore Egypt's greatness and so made the prophecy false. But none did. All down the years Egypt's history has been one sorry record of subserviency—to the Romans, to the Moslem Arabs, to the French, and to the British. True, today it enjoys independence, but it is only one of many small nations and rules no territory but its own.

Remarkable indeed was this vision of the future. But it was not the only one recorded by Ezekiel. God revealed to him also the fate of the once powerful seaport and naval base of Tyre.

In the sixth century B.C. this city, located about forty miles north of Mount Carmel on the Mediterranean coast, wielded an immense influence throughout Asia Minor and Palestine. Its ships roamed the seas as far as Spain, and possibly England.

When Jerusalem fell to the Babylonians there was

great rejoicing in Tyre. On hearing of it Ezekiel wrote: "Thus saith the Lord God; Behold, I am against thee, O Tyrus, and will cause many nations to come up against thee, as the sea causeth his waves to come up. And they shall destroy the walls of Tyrus, and break down her towers: I will also scrape her dust from her, and make her like the top of a rock. It shall be a place for the spreading of nets in the midst of the sea." Ezekiel 26:3-5.

Were the people of Tyre concerned? Not in the least. They were too busy with their commerce to bother about what some "fanatical" Hebrew was saying about them. What power on earth could ever capture their impregnable fortress and scrape it bare "like the top of a rock"?

Then came Nebuchadnezzar. For thirteen years he laid siege to Tyre. So hard did his soldiers labor at the battering rams that "every shoulder was peeled." Ezekiel 29:18. Finally that portion of the city which had been built on the mainland fell to the invaders. But despite all their efforts they could not capture the island, half a mile offshore.

After Nebuchadnezzar's departure many Tyrians no doubt consoled themselves that, while they had suffered great damage, their main city remained inviolate and Ezekiel's prediction had failed.

But it hadn't. God is long on time. He can afford to wait.

Some two hundred forty years later, in 332 B.C., another conqueror approached. This time it was Alexander the Great. With massive forces he soon subdued the rebuilt mainland city, but, like Nebuchadnezzar, he was baffled by the wide stretch of water between him and his main prize. Then he decided upon a most unusual course. Demolishing the mainland city, he literally scraped it bare, using the rubble to build a causeway two hundred feet wide across the straits. At the farther end of this he erected towers and war engines and prepared for the final assault. He was now joined by the king of Cyprus, who arrived with two hundred twenty warships, and the reduction of the fortress was soon accomplished. After a seven months' siege Tyre was taken, with fearful slaughter of the inhabitants.

Alexander's mole may still be seen today. Broken pillars from the once-famous city strew the beaches: Fishermen from the village of Sur spread their nets upon the bare rocks from which the dust of Tyre was scraped by the famous Greek conqueror nearly twenty-three centuries ago.

Thus again God demonstrated the completeness of His knowledge of the future. Only Someone with supernatural vision could have described Tyre's fate in such astonishingly accurate detail.

One more illustration must suffice at this juncture, and this from the greatest prophet of all.

While talking with His disciples in the temple one day, Jesus shocked them by saying, "You see all these buildings? I tell you this: not one stone will be left upon another; all will be thrown down." Matthew 24: 2, N.E.B.

When would this happen?

"When you see Jerusalem encircled by armies, then

you may be sure that her destruction is near. Then those who are in Judea must take to the hills; those who are in the city itself must leave it, and those who are out in the country must not enter; because this is the time of retribution." Luke 21:20-23, N.E.B.

Then He added this even more remarkable prediction: "Jerusalem will be trampled down by foreigners until their day has run its course." Verse 24.

Everything came about exactly as Jesus said. In A.D. 66 Roman armies attacked the city, but then withdrew, thus giving those who remembered Christ's warning a chance to escape. Four years later, A.D. 70, the Romans returned, captured the city, and utterly destroyed it. In their mad search for hidden treasure and their eagerness to salvage the precious metals that flowed in molten streams from the burning buildings, they took the whole place apart, stone by stone.

Then began the long period of subjection that Jesus so marvelously forecast. Century after century Jerusalem was "trampled down by foreigners," or, as the King James Version says, "trodden down of the Gentiles." It was trampled by the Romans, the Moslem Arabs, the Turks. Even today, despite the existence of the new nation of Israel, the ancient city is still in the hands of "foreigners," while a Mohammedan structure stands upon the site of Solomon's temple.

Well did one famous preacher write: "So long as Babylon is in heaps; so long as Nineveh lies empty, void, and waste; so long as Egypt is the basest of kingdoms; so long as Tyre is a place for the spreading of nets in the midst of the sea; so long as Israel is scattered among all nations; so long as Jerusalem is trodden underfoot of the Gentiles; so long as the great empires of the world march on in their predicted course,—so long we have proof that one omniscient mind dictated the predictions of that Book [the Bible] and 'prophecy came not in old time by the will of man.'"—H. L. Hastings, *Will the Old Book Stand?* page 19.

Once this fact is established, once we know for sure that God knows the future as He does the past, our outlook upon the world and all its tumultuous happenings can never be the same. For if it is indeed true that God can declare "new things" "before they spring forth," if, in every circumstance, every historical development, He can see "the end from the beginning," there can be no reason for anxiety or despair. All we need to do is to trust His infinite knowledge, wisdom, power, and love, and leave everything to Him.

Thus as the gathering storm bursts upon us our hearts may be at peace, filled with courage from above, knowing all will come right in the end.

7

PLANS
FOR ETERNITY

NOT only does God know the future, He plans for it. And the evidence of His concern for what is going to happen to this world and its inhabitants is another source of courage in these troubled times.

Far back at history's dawn, when He "formed the earth and made it, . . . He created it not in vain, He formed it to be inhabited." Isaiah 45:18.

He was thinking of its future then, and has been ever since.

When it became necessary to punish the antediluvians for their wickedness, He found a righteous man and told him what He was going to do.

"And God said unto Noah, The end of all flesh is come before Me; for the earth is filled with violence through them; and, behold, I will destroy them with the earth. Make thee an ark." Genesis 6:13, 14.

He foresaw the Flood and made provision for the deliverance of those who wanted to be saved.

Then when the Flood receded and Noah and his family descended from the ark, God was still looking ahead: "I will not again curse the ground," He said. "Neither will I again smite any more everything living, as I have done. While the earth remaineth, seedtime and harvest, and cold and heat, and summer and winter, and day and night shall not cease." Genesis 8: 21, 22.

That was when He made the first rainbow. And as Noah and his family gazed up at the glorious sight, God said to them, "I do set My bow in the cloud, and it shall be for a token of a covenant between Me and the earth. And it shall come to pass, when I bring a cloud over the earth, that the bow shall be seen in the cloud: and I will remember My covenant, which is between Me and you and every living creature of all flesh; and the waters shall no more become a flood to destroy all flesh." Genesis 9:13-15.

In the next verse He says that the rainbow will ever remind Him of His "everlasting covenant"—which suggests He was looking a long, long way ahead just then. Even today the darkest clouds make the backdrop for the most beautiful rainbows, telling us that God still cares for His creatures and that somewhere, not far away, His sun is shining.

Some three centuries after the Flood, when degeneration had again set in, God called Abram to leave the city of Ur of the Chaldees and go to Palestine to found a new nation.

"Get thee out of thy country, and from thy kindred, and from thy father's house, unto a land that I will show thee," was the divine command. The promise followed: "I will make of thee a great nation, and I will bless thee, and make thy name great; and thou shalt be a blessing: . . . and in thee shall all families of the earth be blessed." Genesis 12:1-3.

Notice again the forward look—God's knowledge of the future and His planning for it. Observe also the mingling of His over-all purpose for the world with His personal purpose for Abraham. Though separate, they were completely intertwined, linking Abraham's life with God's; his plans with God's plans. Thus as he set out obediently for Canaan he found himself, before his journey's end, looking "for a city which hath foundations, whose builder and maker is God." Hebrews 11:10.

When Abraham's great-grandson Joseph was sold as a slave into Egypt, it seemed a disaster. Yet it wasn't. It was merely a part of a divine plan, or, as we sometimes say, God's overruling providence. A few years later this same young man, now governor of Egypt, told his brothers who had done the cruel deed:

"Do not be distressed, or angry with yourselves, because you sold me here; for God sent me before you to preserve life. . . . So it was not you who sent me here, but God." Genesis 45:5-8, R.S.V.

It was the same when the time came for Israel to be delivered from Egyptian bondage. Again a plan was needed to meet a truly desperate situation, and God was ready with one.

This time He needed a godly mother, a well-cared-for baby, a devoted sister, and a kindly princess, and they were all there on location, on time. Furthermore, His plans for their individual lives so blended with His eternal purpose that the upshot was the Exodus and freedom for a million people.

Centuries later, when the seventy-year Babylonian captivity was drawing to a close, similar activity was in evidence. In this case even the heathen king who was to pronounce the decree of liberation was named before he was born. Isaiah tells the story: "Thus saith the Lord to His anointed, to Cyrus, whose right hand I have holden, to subdue nations before him: . . . For Jacob My servant's sake, and Israel Mine elect, I have even called thee by thy name: I have surnamed thee, though thou hast not known Me." Isaiah 45:1-4.

Cyrus was the Persian king who first told the Jews they were free to return to their homeland—just seventy years after Nebuchadnezzar had taken them captive. And it was probably the aged prophet Daniel, who was at Babylon's fall the "third ruler in the kingdom" (Daniel 5:29), who brought to his attention Isaiah's two-hundred-year-old prediction.

Thus marvelously does God plan for every emergency. Not even the slightest detail is overlooked. Nothing He plans and promises ever fails to come to pass. Joshua 23:14.

When the time came for Jesus to be born the event found the whole universe activated to make sure that God's supreme plan should be carried out to perfection. Angels swept earthward to alert the shepherds and form the star that guided the wise men from the east.

The *place* had been pinpointed. It had to happen in Bethlehem, as God had foretold through the prophet Micah: "But thou, Bethlehem Ephratah, though thou be little among the thousands of Judah, yet out of thee shall He come forth unto Me that is to be Ruler in Israel; whose goings forth have been from of old, from everlasting." Micah 5:2.

The *time* had been set with equal deliberation by the prophecy in Daniel 9:25: "Know therefore and understand, that from the going forth of the commandment to restore and to build Jerusalem unto the Messiah the Prince shall be seven weeks, and threescore and two weeks."*

And, of course, the *manner* of this epochal birth had been described seven centuries before by Isaiah: "A virgin shall conceive, and bear a Son, and shall call His name Immanuel." Isaiah 7:14.

In amazing detail God foresaw the coming of this Holy Child. Of all events in history this was the most meticulously planned.

Grown to manhood, Jesus revealed similar vision and purpose. He, too, was always looking ahead. As His brief ministry drew to a close He assured His disciples that His departure would be all for their good.

*See Chapter 11.

"Set your troubled hearts at rest," He said to them. "Trust in God always; trust also in Me. There are many dwelling places in My Father's house; if it were not so I should have told you; for I am going there on purpose to prepare a place for you. And if I go and prepare a place for you, I shall come again and receive you to Myself, so that where I am you may be also." John 14:1-3, N.E.B.

He went away "on purpose." He will return "on purpose." Always He has a purpose, a plan to carry out.

Often He carried the disciples' minds forward to that happy day when He will return, not as a Babe in a manger, but as King of kings and Lord of lords, "coming in a cloud with power and great glory." Luke 21:27. He even told the high priest who sat in judgment on Him: "Hereafter shall ye see the Son of man sitting on the right hand of power, and coming in the clouds of heaven." Matthew 26:64.

As He looked still further ahead to the final day of judgment He told how "the Son of man shall come in His glory, and all the holy angels with Him" and He shall sit "upon the throne of His glory: and before Him shall be gathered all nations." In that day, He said, those who have been faithful to Him will hear these words of welcome: "Come, ye blessed of My Father, inherit the kingdom prepared for you from the foundation of the world." Matthew 25:31-34.

What a revelation was this! The ultimate reward of the righteous was conceived in the mind of God "from the foundation of the world." It was planned from the very beginning, before Adam was created!

Even in that far-distant time, so remote that we cannot imagine it, God was looking ahead, planning for the final triumph of good over evil and a wonderful future for all who love Him.

As the apostle Paul wrote to the Corinthians: "Eye hath not seen, nor ear heard, neither have entered into the heart of man, the things which God hath prepared for them that love Him." 1 Corinthians 2:9.

John, the beloved disciple, was given a glimpse of what is in store for the redeemed, and reported seeing a land of beauty and loveliness beyond compare; a land of exquisite happiness and unalloyed bliss; a land where "there shall be no more death, neither sorrow, nor crying, neither shall there be any more pain." Revelation 21:4.

Thus all along God has been planning far into the future, planning for eternity. And His concern for this world and its people over so long a time should inspire us with confidence in His personal interest in us today. His thoughtfulness reaches through and past the gathering storm to the glorious afterward, whose realization has from time immemorial been His supreme obsession.

Because His plans will not, cannot, fail, we may greet the coming crisis with a cheer. Let the storm strike! Let the wild winds blow! What matter? God knows what lies beyond. And He will lead us there.

8

VOICE
IN THE DARK

SOME years ago an old
Christian friend sent me a letter full of good counsel,
concluding with the inspiring exhortation, "Cheer
everybody on!"

Those three words were typical of the man's life and
character. If he had any troubles or ailments of his
own he never mentioned them, being concerned only
with other people's happiness. Gripping your hand
and looking into your eyes as though you were the
best friend he had in the world, he would say, "Courage, brother!" and the radiance of his presence would
last for days.

God is like that. He talks courage, especially when

days are dark, trials are heavy, storm clouds lower, or some difficult and dangerous task needs to be done.

Thirty-five centuries ago an old man of eighty was tending sheep in the wild country of the Sinai Peninsula. His spirit was crushed. Though once heir to the throne of Egypt, he was now a penniless shepherd. He had blundered badly and thrown away what had seemed a golden opportunity. Now he saw nothing ahead but endless wanderings in this wilderness.

Suddenly the silence of days, weeks, and months was broken by a Voice. Someone was there with him in that vast loneliness! Someone who knew his name; Someone who wanted to talk to him.

"Moses! Moses!" called the Voice.

It was the voice of God, speaking from the bush that burned but was not consumed.

"Come now," He said, "and I will send thee unto Pharaoh." Exodus 3:10. See also verses 4-9.

Moses declined. He felt totally inadequate for such a task.

"I'm no good," he said in effect. "I can't talk. Send somebody else."

Then began that long and almost incredible argument between God and a man, with God trying to cheer the man's heart and rekindle the flame of courage in his heart.

"Certainly I will be with thee," He said, later adding this sevenfold assurance:

"Say unto the children of Israel, I am the Lord, and I *will* bring you out from under the burdens of the Egyptians, and I *will* rid you out of their bondage, and I *will* redeem you with a stretched-out arm, and with great judgments: and I *will* take you to Me for a people, and I *will* be to you a God. . . . And I *will* bring you in unto the land, concerning the which I did swear to give it to Abraham, to Isaac, and to Jacob; and I *will* give it you for an heritage: I am the Lord." Exodus 6:6-8.

It was as though He had said, "Courage, Moses, courage! You have nothing to fear. Go on!"

Finally God prevailed, and Moses, albeit with reluctance, strode back toward Egypt.

Every step of the way the Voice behind him said, "Courage!" And he surely needed it. Arriving in Egypt, he had trouble with his own people; they didn't want him for their leader. He had trouble with Pharaoh, who flatly refused his proposals for evacuation. Again and again his efforts seemed to end in failure. But always the Voice said, "Courage! Keep going!"

It was like this all the way to Canaan. Especially at the Red Sea.

Within hours after leaving Egypt it became obvious that he had maneuvered the refugees into the worst possible situation. With mountains on one side and the sea ahead, they were at the mercy of the advancing Egyptians.

Night was falling. Panic was spreading. Cries of terror rose from the camp. The whole Exodus seemed about to collapse.

Moses turned to God. What should he do?

The Voice spoke again.

"Why do you cry to Me?" God asked. "Tell the

people of Israel to go forward." Exodus 14:15, R.S.V.

It was time for action, not for prayer.

"Lift up your rod, and stretch out your hand over the sea and divide it," God ordered. Verse 16.

What courage it took to do that!

Then came the wind. A wild, howling, tempestuous wind, that filled the air with sand, sent clouds hurtling across the sky, and slowly but surely cut a path through the sea.

It was a sight to frighten the boldest heart. Especially those foaming, white-crested walls of water which marked the path ahead.

Silhouetted against the feeble light of dawn Moses, his beard and robe buffeted by the gale, waved and called to the people. They couldn't hear what he said for the sound of the wind and waves, but somehow they guessed his message. It was Courage! Forward!

And forward they went, their terrors quelled by one man's exuberant gallantry.

Forty years later, his task accomplished, Moses prepared to relinquish the leadership of Israel to a younger man. Joshua was his chosen successor, and "in the sight of all Israel" he said to him: "Be strong and of a good courage. . . . Fear not, neither be dismayed."

He had come a long way from the burning bush, this man who had once been so full of fears!

As for Joshua, he was awed by the prospect of having to follow in the footsteps of so great a man. A thousand doubts and fears crowded into his mind.

67

Would the burden be too heavy for him? Would the people obey him as they had obeyed Moses? How could he hope to capture the mountain strongholds of Palestine with this undisciplined crowd?

Then he, too, heard the voice of God. And what a message of courage the Lord had for him!

"As I was with Moses," He said, "so I will be with thee: I will not fail thee, nor forsake thee. Be strong and of a good courage. . . . Only be thou strong and very courageous. . . .

"Have not I commanded thee? Be strong and of a good courage; be not afraid, neither be thou dismayed: for the Lord thy God is with thee whithersoever thou goest." Joshua 1:2-9.

Inspired by this glorious message, Joshua spoke to the people like a man transformed. "Prepare you victuals," he ordered; "for within three days ye shall pass over this Jordan." Verse 11.

They did. His spirit was irresistible. Even the river itself disappeared. And no wonder!

Through all the dark and trying days ahead the voice of God kept breathing, "Courage!" until at last the land was conquered and the occupation completed.

It is wonderfully comforting to know that the same God who sits upon a throne "high and lifted up" cares so much about what His creatures are doing on this earth that He will even whisper courage in their ears when they need it! He is not an "absentee landlord" who has forgotten us. He is not a monarch who lives far off in splendid isolation, but a Friend who is "closer than breathing, nearer than hands or feet."

Many have heard His voice in moments of discouragement and great need.

There was Elijah, a mighty man of God if ever there was one. Undaunted, he bore his witness for righteousness and truth in the days of King Ahab, working spectacular miracles in the name of the Lord. He even brought fire from heaven on Mount Carmel, in the sight of all Israel. But the strain was too much for him. The nervous tension, coupled with the restricted diet on which, like everybody else, he had been forced to live during the three-year famine, finally brought him low. Then it was that, hearing that Queen Jezebel sought his life, he fled to the wilderness a broken, dejected man.

Like so many of us today, he plunged suddenly from the heights to the depths. Though he had just seen God answer his prayer by fire, he was now sure that His cause was lost and that there was no use holding on any longer. "I, even I only, am left," he wailed; "and they seek my life, to take it away." 1 Kings 19:14.

His courage couldn't have sunk lower.

Then, suddenly, the wind rose, increasing to a hurricane of tremendous force, picking up giant rocks and hurling them against each other till they smashed in pieces before his eyes.

As he watched in wonderment, the whole mountain began to shake as though some giant hand were tossing it to and fro. Then from the gaping fissures leaped flaming tongues of fire—all symbols of vast powers beyond Elijah's understanding or control.

With equal suddenness the wind died away, the

mountain ceased to quake, and the fire went out.

Out of the silence came a voice, "a still, small voice." It was the voice of God.

"Go, return!" God said, outlining the tasks still to be done and assuring Elijah that, far from his being alone, there were seven thousand others who had not bowed the knee to Baal. He had no reason to be depressed. The Omnipotent One, who had power over the wind, the earthquake, and the fire, was his Friend and Helper. He must go back and complete his task.

It was as though God had said, "Courage, Elijah! Cheer up! You're not finished yet!"

And he wasn't. Not by any means. He did not know it, but awaiting him were a chariot of fire and the open gates of heaven.

Almost at the same time Jehoshaphat, king of Judah, learned that the people of Ammon, Moab, and Mount Seir were preparing to invade his country. A vast army was already on its way. Caught totally unprepared, and feeling utterly helpless, he took the matter to God.

Kneeling with bowed head in the temple, he cried, "O Lord God of our fathers, art not Thou God in heaven? and rulest not Thou over all the kingdoms of the heathen? and in Thine hand is there not power and might, so that none is able to withstand Thee? . . . O our God, . . . we have no might against this great company that cometh against u‚; neither know we what to do: but our eyes are upon Thee." 2 Chronicles 20:6-12.

It was a dark hour indeed. Everybody was desperately worried, as well they might be, as they "stood before the Lord, with their little ones, their wives, and their children." Verse 13.

Again out of the dark came the voice of God, radiating courage.

"Be not afraid nor dismayed by reason of this great multitude," was His thrilling message; "for the battle is not yours, but God's." Verse 15.

They would not have to fight. God would care for everything. They would only need to "stand . . . still, and see the salvation of the Lord."

So Jehoshaphat "appointed singers unto the Lord," to "praise the beauty of holiness, as they went out before the army, and to say, Praise the Lord; for His mercy endureth forever." Verse 21.

The result was spectacular. Whether or not it was caused by the singing, the Bible does not say. But the enemy suddenly broke and fled, the diverse groups fighting and killing each other. So Jehoshaphat and his people returned to Jerusalem "with psalteries and harps and trumpets unto the house of the Lord"— the very place where they had prayed for help a few short hours before. Their courage was never stronger. They had seen God in action, and their despair had turned to joy.

Toward the end of the first century A.D. the apostle John heard the same voice of encouragement in a dark and evil hour.

A lifetime of witness for his Lord and Master had made him a famous leader in the new and growing church. As such he had incurred the displeasure of the Roman authorities and been banished to Patmos, a barren, volcanic island in the Aegean Sea.

Now, old and tired, he had nothing to do but sit and think of the past, and wonder why everything had gone so wrong.

His years of companionship with Jesus had once filled him with high hope—especially the Master's promise to return in power and glory. He recalled the days of sweet fellowship in Galilee, the exciting episodes in the temple, the opposition of the unbelieving Jews, and finally Calvary, the tomb, and the resurrection. He especially recalled the resurrection—and how Jesus had stayed with His disciples for forty days thereafter. He remembered the ascension, too, and how two angels had appeared and said, "This same Jesus, which is taken up from you into heaven, shall so come in like manner as ye have seen Him go into heaven." Acts 1:11.

Six decades had passed since then, and still Jesus had not returned. Meanwhile the worst had happened. James had been killed. Peter had been crucified. Paul had been beheaded. Eleven of the twelve disciples were in their graves. Only John was left, and he but one short step from his.

No word, no sign had come from heaven. Nothing but silence. Sixty years of silence. Could there have been a mistake? Had he been deceived? Had he preached in vain?

Then all of a sudden he heard "a great voice, as of a trumpet."

It seemed to come from behind him and, turning, he looked into the face of "One like unto the Son of man." Revelation 1:10, 13. There could be no doubt about it. Though His hair was now "white as white wool, white as snow," His eyes "like a flame of fire," His feet "like burnished bronze," and His voice "like the sound of many waters," beyond question it was the same dear Jesus he had known so well in the long ago. Verses 14, 15, R.S.V.

Overjoyed, John fell at his Master's feet. Gently Jesus laid His hand on the old gray head, saying, "Fear not; I am the First and the Last: I am He that liveth, and was dead; and, behold, I am alive forevermore, Amen; and have the keys of hell and of death." Verses 17, 18.

It was as though He said, "John, you are not the last of those who founded My church. I am. And as long as I live My cause is not lost. Death may have taken Peter and James and all the rest. Death may take you. Never mind. *I* am alive forevermore. I have the keys of death. Someday I shall open the graves of all who believe in Me. I am Alpha and Omega, the First and the Last. I was there at the beginning of the battle with evil. I shall be there at the end. The final victory will be Mine. Cheer up! There's no reason to be downhearted. Hold fast your faith. I shall not fail you."

Scales dropped from the old man's eyes. Everything came into focus. Now he understood. The divine purpose was clear. New hope, confidence, and courage surged through his soul and he set out to write that crowning masterpiece of the New Testament—Revelation.

It was the voice that made the difference. The voice of Someone who loved, cared, and understood.

Sometimes it is a "still, small voice," sometimes a "voice like a trumpet," but always it is friendly, cheering, inspiring.

As the days grow darker and the storm clouds become more ominous, it is good to know that God is ever close to us, even right behind us, ready to speak the word of courage in the hour of greatest need.

9

STRENGTH FOR TODAY

M ANY people think that Franklin D. Roosevelt invented the phrase "We have nothing to fear but fear itself." They are wrong. Solomon used it first, three thousand years ago. And he got the idea from God.

"Be not afraid of sudden fear," he wrote, "for the Lord shall be thy confidence." Proverbs 3:25, 26.

"In the fear of the Lord is strong confidence," he added, "and His children shall have a place of refuge." Proverbs 14:26.

All down the centuries God has sought to bring courage to the hearts of those who love Him. Because He is the living God, because He is "the same yesterday, and today, and forever" (Hebrews 13:8), because "His understanding is infinite" (Psalm 147:5), and because His kindness is limitless (Isaiah 54:10), He seeks to bring courage and cheer to His people in every age and circumstance.

The Bible is crowded with assurances of His help and comfort in every kind of trouble which might cause fears to arise in the human heart. Though first given to needy people in the long ago, they are still meaningful for us who live in the awesome years of the twentieth century. Backed by the resources of the Omnipotent, they afford strength for today and hope for tomorrow.

If we accept them at face value, as God's personal message to us, we shall come to the place where we shall say with David, "I will fear no evil." Psalm 23:4.

There were times in this man's checkered career when he *was* afraid. Very much so. But by trusting God for help in his many trials he was finally able to declare, "I sought the Lord, and He heard me, and delivered me from *all my fears.* . . . This poor man cried, and the Lord heard him, and saved him out of all his troubles." Psalm 34:4-6.

Again: "The Lord is on my side; I will not fear: what can man do unto me?" Psalm 118:6.

Well may we covet such buoyancy of spirit. And we may have it if we so desire. The same trust will bring the same results.

Let us look at some of God's many promises designed to maintain our courage at high pitch no matter what may happen to us.

In Time of Want

After long experience of divine watchcare and help, King David wrote: "O fear the Lord, ye His saints: for there is no want to them that fear Him. The young lions do lack, and suffer hunger: but they that seek the Lord shall not want any good thing." Psalm 34: 9, 10.

Said the prophet Isaiah: "When the poor and needy seek water, and there is none, and their tongue faileth for thirst, I the Lord will hear them, I the God of Israel will not forsake them." Isaiah 41:17.

Again, "Fear not. . . . I will pour water upon him that is thirsty, and floods upon the dry ground." "Fear ye not, neither be afraid." Isaiah 44:2, 3, 8.

Writing to the new Christians of Philippi, the apostle Paul assured them: "My God will supply all your wants out of the magnificence of His riches in Christ Jesus." Philippians 4:19, N.E.B.

In Time of Persecution

Said Jesus: "How blest are those who have suffered persecution for the cause of right; the kingdom of heaven is theirs.

"How blest you are, when you suffer insults and persecution and every kind of calumny for My sake. Accept it with gladness and exultation, for you have a rich reward in heaven." Matthew 5:10-12, N.E.B.

Again, when speaking of the time of trouble to come before His return, He said: "They will set upon you and persecute you. You will be brought before synagogues and put in prison; you will be haled before kings and governors for your allegiance to Me. This will be your opportunity to testify; so make up your minds not to prepare your defense beforehand, because I Myself will give you power of utterance and a wisdom which no opponent will be able to resist or refute. Even your parents and brothers, your relations and friends, will betray you. Some of you will be put to death; and you will be hated by all for your allegiance to Me. But not a hair of your head shall be lost. By standing firm you will win true life for yourselves." Luke 21:12-19, N.E.B.

To the church at Smyrna, which suffered cruelly, He sent this cheering message: "I know your tribulation and your poverty. . . . Do not fear what you are about to suffer. Behold, the devil is about to throw some of you into prison, that you may be tested. . . . Be faithful unto death, and I will give you the crown of life." Revelation 2:9, 10, R.S.V.

In Time of Special Danger

After escaping from the Philistine stronghold of Gath, where he had been in mortal peril (1 Samuel 21), David wrote: "Mine enemies would daily swallow me up: for they be many that fight against me, O Thou Most High. What time I am afraid, I will trust in Thee. . . . In God I have put my trust; I will not fear what flesh can do unto me." Psalm 56:2-4.

Again he wrote: "The angel of the Lord encampeth round about them that fear Him, and delivereth them." Psalm 34:7.

This was remarkably fulfilled in Elisha's experience in Dothan, when the king of Syria surrounded the village with troops, hoping to capture the troublesome prophet. Awakening to discover horses and chariots completely encircling their hideout, Elisha's servant cried out in terror, "Alas, my master! how shall we do?"

"Fear not," said Elisha: "for they that be with us are more than they that be with them." 2 Kings 6:16.

Then he prayed, "Lord, . . . open his eyes, that he may see. And the Lord opened the eyes of the young man; and he saw: and, behold, the mountain was full of horses and chariots of fire round about Elisha." Verse 17.

How God's protecting chariots prevailed and how Elisha led the Syrian army to Samaria instead of Damascus is one of the most inspiring of all Bible stories.

Sustaining this revelation of God's protection of those who love and serve Him is this precious promise: "Fear not: for I have redeemed thee, I have called thee by thy name; thou art Mine. When thou passest through the waters, I will be with thee; and through the rivers, they shall not overflow thee: when thou walkest through the fire, thou shalt not be burned; neither shall the flame kindle upon thee. For I am the Lord thy God, the Holy One of Israel, thy Saviour." Isaiah 43:1-3.

While this promise was first made to the people of Israel, it may be claimed by anyone who trusts Him today. Years ago I saw it fulfilled in a most unforgettable way.

When a young man I went to the Western Isles of Scotland selling a book called *Bible Readings for the Home Circle* to raise funds to pay my way through a Christian college. To save money I decided to cross from one island to another on foot, at low tide. It was only a mile or so, and I felt sure there was no danger. All went well until I was halfway across. Then the tide turned. With incredible speed all the low places in the sand began to fill with water. Soon I was stranded on a rapidly shrinking sand bar with the whole Atlantic, it seemed, roaring in around me.

Claiming the promise, "When thou passest through the waters, I will be with thee," and holding my prospectus high in the air—so that it wouldn't get wet!— I waded into the fast-moving, ever-widening stream in front of me. The water came to my knees, my waist, my neck. I slipped and stumbled in holes in the sand but never quite lost my footing. Then, slowly, as I neared the farther shore, the water became shallower. At last I clambered up the rocks, dripping wet, my precious book still dry.

Thus was the promise fulfilled to me. Never shall I forget how I passed through the overflowing waters in safety.

In Public Service

God is aware of the special trials that come to those who seek to serve others in social, political, or religious capacities. He knows how the very sight of a crowd can bring terror to a speaker's heart.

As Jeremiah began his ministry God said to him,

"Be not afraid of their faces: for I am with thee to deliver thee, saith the Lord." "Be not dismayed at their faces. . . . For, behold, I have made thee this day a defensed city, and an iron pillar, and brazen walls against the whole land, against the kings, . . . princes, . . . priests, . . . and . . . people." Jeremiah 1:8, 17, 18.

To Ezekiel He sent a similar message: "I have made thy face strong against their faces. . . . As an adamant harder than flint have I made thy forehead: fear them not, neither be dismayed at their looks." Ezekiel 3:8, 9.

God stands ready to make all His witnesses, in every generation, brave and fearless.

When Meeting Opposition

To Isaiah who, like all the prophets of old, met great opposition, came this inspiring message: "Fear ye not the reproach of men, neither be ye afraid of their revilings. For the moth shall eat them up like a garment, and the worm shall eat them like wool: but My righteousness shall be forever, and My salvation from generation to generation." Isaiah 51:7, 8.

How this promise was fulfilled in the experience of Zerubbabel, as he sought to rebuild the temple following the Babylonian captivity, is another of the great stories of Holy Scripture.

Scarcely had he begun the work than "the people of the land weakened the hands of the people of Judah, and troubled them in building, and hired counselors against them, to frustrate their purpose." Ezra 4:4, 5. They even sent false charges to the king of Persia, who ordered the work to cease.

Then came this electrifying word from the Lord through the prophet Haggai: "Yet now be strong, O Zerubbabel, saith the Lord; and be strong, O Joshua, son of Josedech, the high priest; and be strong, all ye people of the land, saith the Lord, and work: for I am with you, saith the Lord of hosts: . . . My Spirit remaineth among you: fear ye not." Haggai 2:4, 5.

Through Zechariah, who labored with Haggai, came another message of encouragement for the hard-pressed leader:

"This is the word of the Lord unto Zerubbabel, saying, Not by might, nor by power, but by My Spirit, saith the Lord of hosts. Who art thou, O great mountain? before Zerubbabel thou shalt become a plain: and he shall bring forth the headstone thereof with shoutings, crying, Grace, grace, unto it. . . . The hands of Zerubbabel have laid the foundation of this house; his hands shall also finish it." Zechariah 4:6-9.

That is how it turned out. The people worked like men inspired. As they did so the mountains of difficulty dissolved away. In an amazingly short time the headstone was placed in position amid great rejoicing as Zerubbabel saw the task he had begun in faith completed.

When Feeling Crushed

Into everyone's life come times of bitter disappointment and crushing loss. But God has left on record a beautiful promise to meet these special needs.

Through Isaiah He said, "Fear thou not; for I am with thee: be not dismayed; for I am thy God: I will strengthen thee; yea, I will help thee; yea, I will uphold thee with the right hand of My righteousness. . . . For I the Lord thy God will hold thy right hand, saying unto thee, Fear not; I will help thee. Fear not, thou worm Jacob; . . . I will help thee, saith the Lord." Isaiah 41:10-14.

It is the use of the word "worm" that makes this promise so wonderful. God knows when we are that "low;" when we feel wretched and frustrated; when we think everybody around us is trying to step on us and crush us. And He has a message for the "worm" in the verses that follow.

"I will make thee a new sharp threshing instrument having teeth"—which is something a worm never had.

"Thou shalt thresh the mountains, and beat them small, and shalt make the hills as chaff"—which is something a worm never does.

"Thou shalt fan them, and the winds shall carry them away"—which no worm in history ever had the capacity to do. Verse 15, 16.

What a worm!

God gives the poor thing teeth that it may become a threshing instrument.

God gives it power to thresh mountains and beat them small.

God gives it wings to fan the chaff and blow it away till mountains and hills disappear.

Wonderful promise! Read it when you feel "down and out." Your outlook will be completely changed. As Isaiah said, "Thou shalt rejoice in the Lord, and shalt glory in the Holy One of Israel." Verse 16.

In Time of War

Whether fought with bows and arrows, or guns, tanks, and H-bombs, war is always a harsh, cruel, disturbing experience, bringing loss and suffering to victors and vanquished alike. None knew its fears more than David, who lived much of his life in its shadow. His twenty-seventh psalm tells how he kept his heart at peace amid the endless turmoil:

"The Lord is my light and my salvation; whom shall I fear? the Lord is the strength of my life; of whom shall I be afraid? When the wicked, even mine enemies and my foes, came upon me to eat up my flesh, they stumbled and fell. Though an host should encamp against me, my heart shall not fear: though war should rise against me, in this will I be confident. . . . For in the time of trouble He shall hide me in His pavilion: in the secret of His tabernacle shall He hide me; He shall set me up upon a rock." Verses 1-5.

The constant upheaval in which much of his life was spent would have been too much for him but for his unshakable confidence in God. "I had fainted," he said, "unless I had believed to see the goodness of the Lord in the land of the living. Wait on the Lord: be of good courage, and He shall strengthen thine heart: wait, I say, on the Lord." Verses 13, 14.

Confirming this good counsel, Isaiah tells this story from another chapter in Israel's turbulent history:

During the first half of the eighth century B.C. news reached King Ahaz of Judah that an unholy alliance had been formed between the kings of Israel and Syria for his undoing. The allied armies were in fact already on their way to Jerusalem. King Ahaz was so scared that his heart "moved, . . . as the trees of the wood are moved with the wind." Then Isaiah came on the scene with this message from the Lord: "Take heed, and be quiet; fear not, neither be fainthearted for the two tails of these smoking firebrands." Isaiah 7:2, 4.

The Revised Standard Version makes his message tenfold stronger: "Take heed, be quiet, do not fear, and do not let your heart be faint because of these two smoldering stumps of firebrands."

In God's opinion that was all the enemy amounted to. The two kings leading the invasion were nothing but burnt-out firebrands. In a little while their fire would go out, their power be gone.

Regarded in this light most conquerors lose much of their fearsomeness. We should never let our hearts grow faint because of men who, despite all their braggadocio, are naught but "smoldering stumps of firebrands." Calmly waiting on the Lord, trusting confidently in Him, we can be quiet within, knowing their day is almost done.

"You will hear of wars and rumors of wars," said Jesus; "see that you are not alarmed." Matthew 24:6, R.S.V.

In Time of Disaster

In this present evil world we must not be dismayed if disasters of various kinds occur from time to time. "Nation shall rise against nation, and kingdom against kingdom: and there shall be famines, and pestilences, and earthquakes, in divers places." Matthew 24:7.

Will God forget us in these worst of times? Will our source of courage be cut off?

No indeed. When our need is greatest God will be nearest. As He said through the prophet Isaiah: "The mountains may depart and the hills be removed, but My steadfast love shall not depart from you." Isaiah 54:10, R.S.V.

David was right when he declared with glorious positiveness: "God is our refuge and strength, a very present help in trouble. Therefore will not we fear, though the earth be removed, and though the mountains be carried into the midst of the sea." Psalm 46: 1, 2.

When the Gathering Storm Breaks

Let us not deceive ourselves. *Everybody* is not going to be courageous when this happens. There will be many very frightened people in that day.

Men's hearts will fail them for fear, and "for looking after those things which are coming on the earth." Luke 21:26.

They will be "fainting with fear and with foreboding," says the Revised Standard Version.

They will be "swooning with panic and foreboding," according to Dr. Moffatt's translation.

They will "faint with terror," says the New English Bible.

Yet not everyone will be afraid. Some will remain courageous, confident in God's love and watchcare to the end.

Said Jesus: "When all this begins to happen, stand upright and hold your heads high, because your liberation is near." Luke 21:28, N.E.B.

That is what He wants us all to do throughout the storm. Stand upright and hold our heads high.

Not fainting with terror, not swooning with panic, not crushed with despair, but standing upright like brave men of God; holding our heads high because we trust in Him.

Centuries ago God sent this dramatic message to Zerubbabel, governor of Judea:

"I will shake the heavens and the earth; and I will overthrow the throne of kingdoms, and I will destroy the strength of the kingdoms of the heathen; and I will overthrow the chariots, and those that ride in them. . . . In that day, saith the Lord of hosts, will I take thee, O Zerubbabel, My servant, the son of Shealtiel, saith the Lord, and I will make thee as a signet: for I have chosen thee, saith the Lord of hosts." Haggai 2:21-23.

Marvelous promise! In the day of final judgment God will make this good man as a "signet"—a ring—upon His finger. There he will be fully protected, sheltered from all harm.

The hand that shakes the universe will keep His children safe!

As for the name, it doesn't have to be Zerubbabel. It could be yours or mine, for this promise, too, is for all who will accept it. Put yours there now and see how it reads. Plain as day is the message: Hold on to God and He will hold on to you!

Sustained by such assurances of divine watchcare, fortified by these glowing streams of courage from above, all of us can face the future without fear.

In so doing we shall discover how true are the inspired words of Isaiah 26:3, 4: "Thou wilt keep him in perfect peace, whose mind is stayed on Thee: because he trusteth in Thee. Trust ye in the Lord forever: for in the Lord Jehovah is everlasting strength."

Part Three

~~~~~~~~~~~~~~~~~~~~~~~~~~~

COURAGE FROM THE CROSS

Christ's death on Calvary was the supreme revelation of God's love for mankind. Surely if He loved us "so" He will watch over and sustain us through the hardest trials ahead.

KEN GUNALL, ARTIST

10

LOVE TO THE UTTERMOST

Of ALL sources of courage none is more potent than the cross of Christ, for it is the crowning revelation of God's love for mankind.

While it is comforting to know that God is omnipotent and can do anything He pleases; while it is reassuring to believe that He is omniscient and knows everything, past, present, and future; to be certain that He is *love*, that every thought He ever had, every deed He ever performed, every purpose He ever conceived, was inspired by love, is to possess the deepest secret of quiet trust and calm endurance.

When we know for sure that somebody loves us, and we love him, or her, we are willing to do anything, suffer anything, endure anything, for that person without question, argument, or self-pity. So it is in our relationship with God. "There is no room for fear in love; perfect love banishes fear." 1 John 4:18, N.E.B.

Calvary removed all possible doubts of God's love. The fact that He was willing to die such a shameful death when He could so easily have escaped it; to put up with such calumny and ridicule when He didn't deserve it; to cry "forgive them" when He could have consumed His tormenters in righteous indignation; all this demonstrated a capacity to love beyond all human comprehension. Here was revealed a love without limit, a love willing to go to any lengths to accomplish its purposes, a love that "beareth all things, believeth all things, hopeth all things, endureth all things." 1 Corinthians 13:7.

True, long before Calvary, God tried to convince men of His love for them.

He began at creation. Was there ever a more beautiful story of a father's love for his children than the placing of Adam and Eve in the Garden of Eden? Surely no multimillionaire could do more for a young couple today than God did for our first parents, providing them with a home of exquisite loveliness and showering upon them blessings innumerable.

When an enemy entered that paradise and spoiled everything, God promised that, despite the tragedy, His concern for their welfare would continue. To the serpent He said: "I will put enmity between you and the woman, and between your seed and her seed; he shall bruise your head, and you shall bruise his heel." Genesis 3:15, R.S.V. His love would watch over them always.

When almost total rebellion made the Flood necessary, it was love that thought about the ark, love that led Noah to build it, and love that preserved it on those wild, tempestuous waters till the judgment was completed.

It was love that painted the first rainbow on the clouds, with its promise that the waters should never again cover the earth.

It was love that called Abram out of Ur of the Chaldees to found a new and godly nation. Why else should God have bothered? Why else should He have cared?

That burning bush Moses saw in the wilderness was ablaze with love as well as fire. Out of the midst of it God said, "I have surely seen the affliction of My people which are in Egypt, and have heard their cry by reason of their taskmasters; for I know their sorrows." Exodus 3:7. Only love could have said that.

It was love that uttered the Ten Commandments on Mount Sinai. The Bible says so: "The Lord came from Sinai: . . . from His right hand went a fiery law for them. Yea, He loved the people." Deuteronomy 33:2, 3.

The chief purpose of those commandments was to inspire love—love to God and love to man.

The first four were compressed by Moses into one brief sentence: "Thou shalt love the Lord thy God with all thine heart, and with all thy soul, and with all thy might." Deuteronomy 6:5.

The last six needed but seven words to encompass them: "Thou shalt love thy neighbor as thyself." Leviticus 19:18. Everyone was to love the deaf, the blind, the poor, the alien, as himself. Verses 14, 15, 34.

Over and over again God reminded the people of His love for them. "The Lord had a delight in thy fathers to love them," said Moses. Deuteronomy 10:15.

On another occasion he confided, "The Lord did not set His love upon you, nor choose you, because ye were more in number than any people; for ye were the fewest of all people: but because the Lord loved you. . . . Know therefore that the Lord thy God, He is God, the faithful God, which keepeth covenant and mercy with them that love Him and keep His commandments to a thousand generations." Deuteronomy 7:7-9.

Even Israel's experience with Balaam was quoted as a token of God's loving care for them. "The Lord thy God turned the curse into a blessing unto thee, because the Lord thy God loved thee." Deuteronomy 23:5.

One of the most beautiful revelations of God's love in the Old Testament is found in Psalm 103, where David says, "The Lord is merciful and gracious, slow to anger, and plenteous in mercy. . . . For as the heaven is high above the earth, so great is His mercy toward them that fear Him." Verses 8-11.

His love is like that of a father: "Like as a father pitieth his children, so the Lord pitieth them that fear Him." Verse 13.

His love is like that of a mother: "As one whom his mother comforteth, so will I comfort you." Isaiah 66:13.

Though brief, Christ's sojourn upon earth was replete with love. From Nazareth to Olivet love poured forth from His tender heart in a ceaseless stream of gentle words and kindly deeds.

His chief joy lies in loving: "I am the Lord which exercise loving-kindness, judgment, and righteousness, in the earth: for in these things I delight, saith the Lord." Jeremiah 9:24.

"Yea, I have loved thee with an everlasting love: therefore with loving-kindness have I drawn thee." Jeremiah 31:3.

Even when sin has separated people from Him, God says with infinite tenderness: "O, . . . return unto the Lord thy God; for thou hast fallen by thine iniquity. Take with you words, and turn to the Lord. . . . I will heal their backsliding, I will love them freely." Hosea 14:1-4.

Thus God was love through all those far-off years. He was love in the Garden of Eden; He was love in the storm-rocked ark; He was love throughout the slavery in Egypt; He was love in the wilderness of Sinai; He was love in the Promised Land; He was love during the Babylonian captivity; and He was love when the people returned to Jerusalem.

Many times His love was spurned, ignored, and rejected, but it did not change. Nor did it lessen. It remained an inexhaustible reservoir waiting to be released someday in all its fullness.

And because God *was* love through all those sad millenniums, and because He *is* love (1 John 4:16) "from everlasting to everlasting," at last He wrapped Himself in a little bundle of human flesh and, in the person of His Son, came to live upon earth as a man.

Thus we read: "God so loved the world that He gave His only Son, that whoever believes in Him should not perish but have eternal life." John 3:16, R.S.V.

God saw that this was the only way to reclaim man from the sad state into which he had fallen; the only way to bring him back into loving fellowship with his Maker.

Man could not restore himself. That was impossible. He had gone too far. He had sunk too low. God must do it for him. He must receive in Himself the penalty He had decreed for sin. Knowing all things, He knew, of course, that it would lead to Calvary; but being love He was willing to go there.

So He came to this earth in the ever-mysterious, ever-glorious Incarnation. "God was in Christ, reconciling the world unto Himself." 2 Corinthians 5:19.

It was a brief sojourn, yet replete with love. All the way from Nazareth to Olivet He sought to convince people of His undying affection for them. From His tender heart love poured forth in a ceaseless stream of gentle words and kindly deeds.

Like the good Samaritan of His own parable He bound up the wounds of His enemies. Graciously He befriended the poor, the sick, the outcast. He loved the children, the young people, the old folks.

Calling a little child to Him, He said to His disciples, "It is not the will of your Father which is in heaven, that one of these little ones should perish." Matthew 18:14.

"Suffer little children to come unto Me," He added, "and forbid them not: for of such is the kingdom of God."

When He met the rich young ruler, the Bible says, "Jesus beholding him loved him." Mark 10:21.

"Behold *how* He loved him!" exclaimed the bystanders as they saw Jesus weeping in sympathy with Mary and Martha over the death of their brother.

Love was the central theme of His teaching. His disciples, He said, were to love not only their friends but also their enemies. They were to do good to those who hated them and pray for those who did them harm. Matthew 5:44.

They were to love God with all their heart, soul, mind, and strength, and their neighbors as themselves. Matthew 22:37-39.

"He that loveth Me," He said, "shall be loved of My Father, and I will love him." John 14:21.

"The Father Himself loveth you," He assured His followers, "because ye have loved Me." John 16:27.

He taught men to call God "Father," which was a new idea to most of them. They had wandered so far away from God that they pictured Him as stern, cruel, and inaccessible. God wasn't like that at all, Jesus said. Instead He was tender, kind, thoughtful, and understanding. "When ye pray," He told them, "say, Our Father which art in heaven." Luke 11:2.

Many people, He suggested, are like a prodigal son who leaves home proudly and self-confidently to enjoy the pleasures of sin. In consequence, they get into much trouble and sorrow. But if they repent and return to God, they will find a loving heavenly Father waiting with outstretched arms to welcome them.

Completing His revelation of the love of God,

99

Jesus went at last to the cross. There, as the Son of God and the one sinless representative of the race, with His divine and human natures inseparably blended, He offered up a complete, perfect, and all-sufficient sacrifice for the sins of men.

Thus was the penalty paid. And "as by one man's disobedience many were made sinners, so by the obedience of One shall many be made righteous." Romans 5:19.

This sacrifice was in no sense intended to appease an angry deity. Rather it was God offering Himself. As we read above, "God so loved . . . that He gave;" and the sharing in this sublime transaction of all Three Persons of the blessed Trinity is revealed in the beautiful words: "Christ . . . through the eternal Spirit offered Himself without spot to God." Hebrews 9:14.

Here indeed was perfect love, made manifest by an act of complete self-surrender and submission, the willing yielding up of life that others might live.

What the Incarnation cost God the Father we shall never know. How much it meant for God the Son to die for the human race must also remain a mystery. Even the angels do not understand it. It will be the theme of endless discussion and wonderment through all eternity. 1 Peter 1:11, 12.

Nevertheless the results are clear.

God "hath made Him to be sin for us, who knew no sin; that we might be made the righteousness of God in Him." 2 Corinthians 5:21.

"Christ redeemed us from the curse of the law, having become a curse for us." Galatians 3:13, R.S.V.

Thus did God seek to bridge the gulf that sin had made. As Peter wrote: "Christ also hath once suffered for sins, the just for the unjust, that He might bring us to God." 1 Peter 3:18.

Contemplating anew this great and glorious deed, this almost incredible act of sublime self-sacrifice and dauntless gallantry, how can we longer entertain doubts or fears concerning the future?

If God *so* loved the world, how great must be His love for us today!

If He loved us *so*, will He not care for us, watch over us, sustain and fortify us through the gathering storm?

"In Christ God has met and overcome the powers of evil and death," says the message issued by the National Council of Churches at its Fifth General Assembly. "In this Event we find the ground of our hope and the assurance of God's final victory. . . .

"It is in gratitude for God's self-offering—gratitude for His supreme act of becoming Immanuel, 'God with us'—that we find resoluteness to oppose iniquity and injustice, compassion to minister to the weak and the suffering, indignation and sympathy as response to prejudice and hatred, fortitude to confront the tasks and hazards of this perilous generation with courage and faith. . . . Thanks be to God for His unspeakable gift!"

Yes indeed. Thanks be to God for Calvary's glorious message in this crisis hour.

11

LINKS IN A GOLDEN CHAIN

*W*E MAY draw courage from the cross not only because it is the crowning evidence of God's love, but also because it is the kingpin in His grand design for man's redemption. As such we may rely upon it with confidence in every time of uncertainty and peril.

Calvary was no accident. It was conceived in the mind of Infinite Wisdom millenniums before it happened. It was planned, arranged, agreed to, far in advance as the only possible solution to the problem of sin. In this sense the Lamb was "slain from the foundation of the world." Revelation 13:8.

When God in His unfathomable love decided to

give freedom of choice to His creatures He knew full well that Calvary would be the only answer to rebellion. Deliberately He took this calculated risk.

Yet though this holy Sacrifice dates back to the dawn of time, it will be remembered through all time to come, for "blessing, and honor, and glory, and power" shall "be unto Him that sitteth upon the throne, and unto the Lamb *forever and ever.*" Revelation 5:13. Thus the cross is the central link in a golden chain binding two eternities, the infinite past with the infinite future. It links Eden lost with Eden restored; the beautiful creation that was spoiled by sin with the glory land of tomorrow where only righteousness shall dwell forevermore. 2 Peter 3:13.

No wonder the prophets wrote about it so frequently! No wonder they described it in such elaborate detail! God intended that there should be no mistake, no misunderstanding, concerning an event of such paramount importance.

Significantly there are more predictions concerning the last few hours of Christ's life on earth than about any other happening mentioned in the Holy Scriptures, except possibly His return in glory.

About 1050 B.C. David described Christ's final agonies in the twenty-second psalm, where he wrote these truly prophetic words: "My God, My God, why hast Thou forsaken Me? Why art Thou so far from helping Me, from the words of My groaning?"

"All who see Me mock at Me; . . . 'He committed His cause to the Lord; let Him deliver Him, let Him rescue Him, for He delights in Him!'"

"They have pierced My hands and feet."

"They divide My garments among them, and for My raiment they cast lots." Psalm 22:1, 7, 8, 16, 18, R.S.V.

About 700 B.C. Isaiah wrote of Christ's sufferings in words of incomparable beauty: "He is despised and rejected of men; a Man of Sorrows, and acquainted with grief. . . . Surely He hath borne our griefs, and carried our sorrows: yet we did esteem Him stricken, smitten of God, and afflicted. But He was wounded for our transgressions, He was bruised for our iniquities: the chastisement of our peace was upon Him; and with His stripes we are healed." Isaiah 53:3-5.

Most remarkable of all, however, is the great time prophecy in the book of Daniel, written around 538 B.C., which sets forth with remarkable clarity the very year in which the crucifixion would occur.

Brief mention has already been made of this, but its vital importance deserves fuller study here.

Note these detailed specifications: "Seventy weeks are determined upon thy people and upon thy Holy City, to finish the transgression, and to make an end of sins, and to make reconciliation for iniquity, and to bring in everlasting righteousness, and to seal up the vision and prophecy, and to anoint the most holy.

"Know therefore and understand, that from the going forth of the commandment to restore and to build Jerusalem unto the Messiah the Prince shall be seven weeks, and threescore and two weeks. . . . And after threescore and two weeks shall Messiah be cut off, but not for Himself. . . .

"And He shall confirm the covenant with many for one week: and in the midst of the week He shall cause the sacrifice and the oblation to cease." Daniel 9:24-27.

In prophecy a day is reckoned as a year. Ezekiel 4:6. Therefore seventy weeks represented 490 years, a period not hard to calculate once the starting date is known.

What event was to mark the beginning of this prediction? "The going forth of the commandment to restore and to build Jerusalem."

When did that happen?

In the year 457 B.C. As a matter of fact, three decrees were issued by Persian rulers to bring about the restoration of Jerusalem, following Israel's captivity in Babylon. The first was by Cyrus in 537 B.C., the second by Darius in 519 B.C., and the third by Artaxerxes in 457 B.C. All three were needed to complete the task, and all three were combined by Ezra in the following significant statement: "And they builded, and finished it, according to the commandment of the God of Israel, and according to the commandment of Cyrus, and Darius, and Artaxerxes king of Persia." Ezra 6:14.

Notice now the division of the seventy weeks into a long period of sixty-nine weeks and a short period of one week.

Sixty-nine weeks, or 483 years, were to reach to "Messiah the Prince."

Subtracting 457 B.C. from 483, one arrives at A.D. 26. But since Artaxerxes' decree was given in the autumn of 457 B.C., the period actually reaches to the autumn

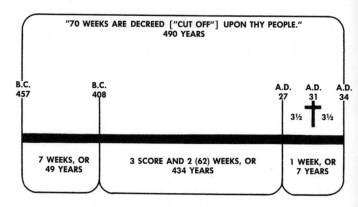

"70 WEEKS ARE DECREED ["CUT OFF"] UPON THY PEOPLE."
490 YEARS

B.C. 457 | B.C. 408 | A.D. 27 | A.D. 31 | A.D. 34

3½ † 3½

7 WEEKS, OR 49 YEARS | 3 SCORE AND 2 (62) WEEKS, OR 434 YEARS | 1 WEEK, OR 7 YEARS

of A.D. 27, which was when Christ entered upon His public ministry as the "Messiah," or Anointed One, at His baptism in the Jordan by John the Baptist. Then it was that He declared, "The time is fulfilled"—the time of this very prediction. Mark 1:15.

God left no loophole for doubt concerning this vital date. He saw to it that Luke, when writing his record of the life of Jesus, made this precise notation: "Now in the fifteenth year of the reign of Tiberius Caesar, Pontius Pilate being governor of Judea, . . . the word of God came unto John the son of Zacharias in the wilderness. And he came into all the country about Jordan, preaching the baptism of repentance for the remission of sins." Luke 3:1-3.

Here are two historical references that can readily be checked: First, the fifteenth year of Tiberius, and second, the governorship of Pontius Pilate. Available evidence indicates rather clearly that the fifteenth year of Tiberius must be placed in A.D. 27-28, while Pilate commenced his governorship in A.D. 26 or early in A.D. 27.

All this is remarkable enough, but the rest is breathtaking. For the prophecy also says: "In the midst of the week [that is, the last of the seventy weeks] He shall cause the sacrifice and the oblation to cease." He shall be "cut off, but not for Himself."

Jesus' ministry lasted precisely three and a half years. Then He was crucified, offering up in Himself "one sacrifice for sins forever" (Hebrews 10:12), thus making all other "sacrifices and oblations" needless. Even as He hung upon the cross "the veil of the temple was rent in twain from the top to the bottom" (Matthew 27:51), as invisible hands thus declared to the ministering priests that their sacrificial ritual was no longer needed.

In that same hour Jesus made "reconciliation for iniquity" by bridging the gulf which sin had made between man and God. He also brought in "everlasting righteousness" by making it possible for all who believe in Him to be "justified freely by His grace" (Romans 3:24) that we "might serve Him without fear, in holiness and righteousness before Him, all the days of our life." Luke 1:74, 75.

As to the last half of the final or seventieth week, this met its fulfillment in the preaching of the gospel exclusively to the Jews during those three and a half years. After the Jewish leaders rejected it, demonstrating their opposition by stoning Stephen and persecuting the church, the cry was raised among the disciples, "Lo, we turn to the Gentiles." Acts 13:46.

Thus were seventy weeks, or 490 years, "determined upon," or assigned to, the Jewish people. The original word *chathak* suggests "to cut" or "to cut off" and is so used in post-Biblical Hebrew, a meaning reflected in the Vulgate *abbreviare*.

And here the full glory of this wonderful prophecy begins to appear. Obviously the seventy weeks were "cut off," or "abbreviated," from something else. From what?

There can be but one answer: From the longer prophetic time period mentioned in the eighth chapter. Both chapters, eight and nine, are intimately related and should always be studied together.

In Daniel 8:13 we read: "I heard one saint speaking, and another saint said unto the wonderful numberer, How long shall be the vision concerning the daily sacrifice, and the transgression of desolation, to give both the sanctuary and the host to be trodden under-foot?" (margin).

Then follows the answer: "Unto two thousand and three hundred days; then shall the sanctuary be cleansed." Verse 14.

As days in prophecy represent years, we have here the longest time prophecy in all the Holy Scriptures: twenty-three hundred years, longer than the whole Christian Era!

Notice now the definite statement that this time prophecy is to reach clear down to the "time of the end."

Said Gabriel, who was commanded by the Lord to

instruct Daniel in this matter, "Understand, O son of man: for at the time of the end shall be the vision." Verse 17.

Dr. Moffatt translates this latter phrase thus: *"It relates to the crisis at the close."*

What a prediction is this—reaching from some point in the distant past down to "the crisis at the close" of human history and the end of the world!

When did this period begin?

There is only one possible starting place: The same as the seventy weeks. These two time periods begin together. They are concurrent for 490 years; then the longer period runs on for another 1810 years until "the crisis at the close."

Taking the starting point as 457 B.C., we are confronted with the startling fact that the 2300-year prophecy extended into the middle of the nineteenth century or, to be precise, to A.D. 1844.

At that time "the crisis at the close" was to begin. Did it? The history of the past 118 years is the answer. What a time of crisis it has been! It has witnessed the greatest wars, famines, pestilences, and earthquakes of all time. It has seen more distress and perplexity, more violence and terrorism, than any other era since man first dwelt upon the earth. Today the Damoclean sword of total nuclear destruction hovers precariously about our heads.

Here we catch a fresh glimpse of the golden chain of which the cross is the central link. For not only does this chain bind Eden lost to Eden restored; not only does it link the eternal past to the eternal future;

it links also Christ's two advents: the first in humility and suffering, the second in power and glory. It links the cross to the crown; the dying Saviour on Calvary to His return as King of kings and Lord of lords.

What rich reserves of courage such knowledge should bring to our fearful hearts! For here is incontrovertible evidence not only of God's love, foreknowledge, and watchcare, but of His precise attendance to detail in the fulfillment of every prophecy concerning His plan for our redemption.

Obviously His concern for this planet and its people is not temporary but permanent, embracing not only the far-distant past and the activities of prophets and apostles long since dead, but also our own times and ourselves.

It spans the ages. Millenniums ago He was thinking of, and planning for, today. Our day. He knew, even then, what would occur in the nineteenth century and the twentieth century. He foresaw "the crisis at the close" and how it would mount in complexity and fury until its climax at Christ's glorious return. And by His revelation of all this through the prophet Daniel He planned to give us courage to meet that crisis undismayed.

Jesus removes all terrors from the day of judgment. When we come face to face with the broken law of God He is our Friend in court, His love canceling every sin of all who trust in Him.

HARRY ANDERSON, ARTIST   © P.P.P.A.

12

FRIEND IN THE HIGHEST COURT

ANOTHER potent source of spiritual fortitude in these trying times is hidden in the twin time prophecies considered in the previous chapter. Here, too, is courage from the cross.

Glance again at the eighth and ninth chapters of the book of Daniel. Note how the 2300 years were to reach not only to "the crisis at the close," but to another event seldom mentioned, rarely understood, and yet of superlative importance.

In answer to the question, "How long shall be the vision?" the answer is given, "Unto two thousand and three hundred days; then shall the sanctuary be cleansed." Daniel 8:13, 14.

What sanctuary did the wonderful numberer have in mind? Certainly not the one in old Jerusalem, for he knew full well that it wouldn't last that long.

To what other sanctuary, then, did he refer? Presumably the one with which he was most familiar, the sanctuary in heaven.

That such a sanctuary exists is clearly stated in the book of Hebrews, where we read: "Now of the things which we have spoken this is the sum: We have such an High Priest, who is set on the right hand of the throne of the Majesty in the heavens; a minister of the sanctuary, and of the true tabernacle, which the Lord pitched, and not man." Hebrews 8:1, 2.

The tabernacle which Moses built in the wilderness was but a tiny miniature of this sanctuary in heaven, the pattern of which was shown to him on Mount Sinai. Verse 5. Of the vastness and magnificence of the original edifice, the dwelling place of the eternal God, no human being can have the faintest concept. We can only accept what is written; that somewhere, at the heart of the infinite universe, there is a place of indescribable beauty and perfect holiness where dwells the Source of all life, wisdom, and power, and where He reigns justly and lovingly over His limitless dominion.

Why speak of cleansing such a place? Surely not because of any sin that might be there. No indeed. No trace of evil could possibly mar its utter purity. But the *record* of sin is there. The Bible says so. In "books" far more wonderful than the latest electronic computers are recorded everything that has ever happened on this earth—all its sins and sorrows, every unworthy deed men have committed, every idle word that they have spoken. Ecclesiastes 12:14; Matthew 12:36. Year after year, century after century, angel hands have "fed" this information into these infinitely complex, infinitely exact, recording devices that are possibly described in the book of Revelation as living creatures "full of eyes within." Revelation 4:8.

God does not plan to preserve this sad record forever. He only needs it to demonstrate to the universe that His final disposition of sin is absolutely just. Then He will dispose of it so completely that the former things "shall not be remembered, nor come into mind." Isaiah 65:17.

Here the old wilderness sanctuary helps us greatly, for its services as well as its structure were fashioned after the heavenly.

In ancient times, when a person committed a sin he had to bring a sacrifice to the tabernacle. Its blood was taken inside and presented before the Lord. Day after day, and many times a day, this process continued, each sacrifice representing, in symbolic form, the transfer of sin to the sanctuary and its recording there.

Then, once a year, a special ceremony was conducted called the "cleansing" of the sanctuary, when, in elaborate ritual, the record of sins was removed and transferred to a "scapegoat," which was taken far from the camp and released to die in the wilderness. Then Israel started a fresh new year, free from all stain and memory of sin.

That day, known as the Day of Atonement, was to the people of Israel the most important and solemn day of the year. "So awful was the Day of Atonement that we are told in a Jewish book of ritual that the very angels run to and fro in fear and trembling, saying, 'Lo, the day of judgment has come!' "—F. W. Farrar, *The Early Days of Christianity*, page 276.

Through all the centuries this impression has remained, and devout Jews in every land on earth still observe Yom Kippur, the Day of Atonement, with the greatest solemnity.

The late Dr. J. H. Hertz, who long held the position of Chief Rabbi of the British Empire, called this day "the most solemn day in the Jewish year," adding, "No other nation, ancient or modern, has an institution approaching the Day of Atonement in religious depth —'a day of purification and of turning from sins, for which forgiveness is granted through the grace of the merciful God, who holds penitence in as high esteem as guiltlessness' (Philo)."—*The Pentateuch and Haftorahs*, notes on Leviticus 23:26-32.

Of this special day *The Jewish Encyclopedia* says: "New Year's and Atonement days are days of serious meditation. . . . The former is the annual day of judgment, . . . when all creatures pass in review before the searching eye of Omniscience."

In the same article the following description of the Day of Atonement is included: "God, seated on His throne to judge the world, . . . openeth the Book of Records; it is read, every man's signature being found therein. The great trumpet is sounded; a still, small voice is heard; the angels shudder, saying, This is the day of judgment. . . . On New Year's Day the decree is written; on the Day of Atonement it is sealed who shall live and who are to die."—Article, "Atonement, Day of."

If this is how the greatest Jewish authorities still regard the Day of Atonement—more than thirty-five centuries after its institution in the wilderness tabernacle—it could well be that the great time prophecy we are here considering has a meaning of epochal importance for our present generation.

If the "cleansing of the sanctuary" is equivalent to the day of judgment, think for a moment of the vast potential in the prophetic words, "Then shall the sanctuary be cleansed."

They can mean but one thing: That A.D. 1844 marked the beginning of "the crisis at the close" in heaven as well as on earth.

The prophet Daniel saw in vision what then took place, describing the sublime, magnificent scene as best he could in human language: "I beheld till the thrones were cast down, and the Ancient of Days did sit, whose garment was white as snow, and the hair of His head like the pure wool: His throne was like the fiery flame, and His wheels as burning fire. A fiery stream issued and came forth from before Him: thousand thousands ministered unto Him, and ten thousand times ten thousand stood before Him: *the judgment was set, and the books were opened.*" Daniel 7:9, 10.

Unnoticed on the earth, never mentioned in the

newspapers of the day, *this* was the supreme event of 1844. And it did not end in that year. Presumably the heavenly court has been in session ever since. It is in session now.

Hence the writing on the wall for so many men and nations: "Weighed in the balances, and . . . found wanting!" Daniel 5:27.

Hence the cry in every land on earth, like the sound of silver trumpets: "Fear God, and give glory to Him; for the hour of His judgment is come." Revelation 14:7.

The "third dimension" of the present crisis thus appears as its most important phase, affecting the future not only of every person alive today, but of all who have ever lived, or shall live, on this planet. God is now choosing its future inhabitants.

But will not the process take all eternity? How could millions upon millions of cases, including everything that everybody has ever said and done, be properly considered and adjusted in any less time?

Let us not limit God.

After all, was it not He who created the brain that invented the electronic computer?

Was it not He who created the mind that first thought of radar, television, microfilm, and all the other amazing devices of our day?

If man can take motion pictures on one side of the world and project them simultaneously on the other, ten thousand miles or more away, surely God could do the same.

If man can record every word of every book written from the time of Christ till now on a few rolls of microfilm, and reproduce them at will, couldn't God do likewise if He should so desire?

And if man can put a hundred thousand cards through an IBM machine in a couple of hours to determine how much employees are to receive for their week's work, couldn't God do something similar in the judgment, when everybody has to be paid in full—and fast?

Of course. God's resources are immeasurable. Nothing is impossible to Him. As Paul wrote to the Romans, "The Lord will execute His sentence upon the earth with rigor and dispatch." Romans 9:28, R.S.V.

But there is another facet of this study that is of particular interest. When Daniel described the judgment scene he added these thrilling words: "I saw in the night visions, and, behold, one like the Son of man came with the clouds of heaven, and came to the Ancient of Days, and they brought Him near before Him. And there was given Him dominion, and glory, and a kingdom, that all people, nations, and languages, should serve Him." Daniel 7:13, 14.

So Jesus is there, in the midst of the judgment scene! As Son of man and Son of God He attends the entire proceedings.

Thus, if you and I have accepted Him as our Saviour we have a Friend in court. And more than a Friend, a Lover, who died on the cross to prove how much He loves us.

Needless, therefore, are any fears. Awesome as the judgment is, Jesus removes its terrors. We may leave our cases confidently in His hands. If we do so, He will care for our interests with the utmost solicitude. He will win for us a favorable verdict. His love will cancel "innumerable sins"—all we ever committed. 1 Peter 4:8, N.E.B.

So from the courts of glory comes yet another word of cheer for this hour of crisis. "Courage!" says Jesus. "The victory is Mine." John 16:33, N.E.B.

It is His—and ours.

13

SETTING THE
WORLD AFIRE

JESUS once said a very strange thing: "I am come to send fire on the earth." Luke 12:49.

"I have come to set fire to the earth," is the rendering of the New English Bible.

What did He mean? That He planned to set fire to the cities of the nations like some pagan conqueror? That He intended to scorch the earth, setting its fields and forests aflame? No indeed. Nothing was further from His thoughts.

What He planned to do was to set the minds and hearts of men afire. To kindle within them a conflagration that would sweep around the globe, leaping over every barrier to human understanding, consuming every cause of strife, and burning up all the trash, folly, and sin that have robbed men of peace and happiness down the years.

What sort of fire could do this?

Love. Pure, unselfish love. God's love.

"God is love," the Bible says. 1 John 4:16. And, "Our God is a consuming fire." Hebrews 12:29.

Love is the strongest force in the universe; stronger than all implements of war, stronger than all the powers of darkness, stronger than hate, stronger than evil. Let it loose and it will sweep on irresistibly to accomplish the sublime purposes of the Almighty.

That is what Jesus did when He went to the cross. He let love loose among men. He touched their hearts with the torch of heaven.

In most cases only a spark was needed—the spark of the glorious concept that "God *so* loved the world" that He was willing to give His own Son to die in man's stead.

John, the youngest of the twelve disciples, was completely carried away with it. "Behold, what manner of love the Father hath bestowed upon us," he wrote, "that we should be called the sons of God." 1 John 3:1.

"Woe to me if I do not preach the gospel!" exclaimed the apostle Paul. 1 Corinthians 9:16, R.S.V. Again, "O the depth of the riches both of the wisdom and knowledge of God! how unsearchable are His judgments, and His ways past finding out!" Romans 11:33.

Fire from the cross had set these men ablaze. The

As the two disciples from Emmaus suddenly recognized Jesus, and He vanished from their sight, they burst into flame for Him crying, "Did not our heart burn within us, while He talked with us by the way?"

love of God in Christ had consumed every selfish purpose they ever had and forged within them one single dedicated purpose.

Thousands had the same experience in those early years of the Christian church.

"Did not our heart burn within us," said the disciples on the Emmaus road, "while He talked with us by the way, and while He opened to us the Scriptures?" Luke 24:32.

Nor was it without significance that "tongues like as of fire" descended upon the 120 believers gathered in the upper room at Pentecost. Each person there became a firebrand for the Lord, while the "rushing mighty wind" (Acts 2:2) fanned the flames till they roared through the market place and the temple and, leaping the walls of Jerusalem, spread through Palestine, Asia Minor, Greece, Macedonia, Italy, and North Africa as those first Christians "preached everywhere, the Lord working with them." Mark 16:20. In their pristine zeal they went forth "conquering, and to conquer" (Revelation 6:2) and almost burned up the Roman Empire.

So hot was the fire of love the cross kindled in some hearts that many were completely transformed by it. They became new men and new women. Old, troublesome dispositions were purged, while latent talents were discovered and fashioned into spiritual weapons of amazing potency. Scrap metal came from this furnace brilliant as stainless steel.

Weak, vacillating Peter, for instance, suddenly found himself preaching to three thousand people with all the skill, poise, and fervor of a seasoned evangelist. Notice how his theme was the cross of Christ:

"Men of Israel, listen to me," he said. "I speak of Jesus of Nazareth, a man singled out by God and made known to you through miracles, portents, and signs, which God worked among you through Him, as you well know. When He had been given up to you, by the deliberate will and plan of God, you used heathen men to crucify and kill Him. But God raised Him to life again, setting Him free from the pangs of death, because it could not be that death should keep Him in its grip." "Let all Israel then accept as certain that God has made this Jesus, whom you crucified, both Lord and Messiah." Acts 2:22-24, 36, N.E.B.

What courage was Peter's now! This man, who but a few weeks before had three times denied knowing Christ, seemed almost reckless in his eagerness to champion His cause.

Brought before the high priest and the council to answer for a disturbance in the temple, he faced his accusers boldly, saying, "Rulers of the people and elders, if the question put to us today is about help given to a sick man, and we are asked by what means he was cured, here is the answer: . . . it was by the name of Jesus Christ of Nazareth, whom you crucified, whom God raised from the dead." Acts 4:9, 10, N.E.B.

When ordered to cease preaching about Christ he replied: "Is it right in God's eyes for us to obey you rather than God? Judge for yourselves. We cannot possibly give up speaking of things we have seen and heard." Verses 19, 20, N.E.B.

Released, he went on preaching, only to be arrested again. Escaping from prison he started once more, right in the temple precincts!

Asked by the high priest why he had disobeyed orders to desist, Peter answered fearlessly, "We must obey God rather than man." Acts 5:30, N.E.B.

As a result, he and his companion John were flogged. But the pain and humiliation did not disturb them. "They departed from the presence of the council, rejoicing that they were counted worthy to suffer shame for His name." Acts 5:41.

Did they stop preaching?

They did not. Instead, "daily in the temple, and in every house, they ceased not to teach and preach Jesus Christ." Verse 42.

Their courage was so extraordinary that it became a subject of discussion among the priests and rulers. The record states that "as they observed the boldness of Peter and John, and noted that they were untrained laymen, they began to wonder, then recognized them as former companions of Jesus." Acts 4:13, N.E.B.

Jesus, they recalled, had manifested similar courage under trial. Strange! What secret did these men have?

It was love. Love for God and love for their fellow men. Love ignited by the cross and now burning like an incandescent flame in their hearts.

They talked about it, and wrote about it, as though it were the one consuming purpose of their lives.

In a general letter to all the early Christians Peter said, "You were ransomed, . . . not with perishable things such as silver or gold, but with the precious blood of Christ, like that of a lamb without blemish or spot." 1 Peter 1:18, 19, R.S.V. Therefore, he pleaded, "love one another earnestly from the heart." Verse 22, R.S.V.

"Put away all malice and all guile and insincerity and envy and all slander," he urged. 1 Peter 2:1, R.S.V. Jesus, he reminded them, set an example of patience and gentleness. "When He was reviled, He did not revile in return; when He suffered, He did not threaten." Verse 23, R.S.V. So, Peter reasoned, we should adorn ourselves "with the imperishable jewel of a gentle and quiet spirit, which in God's sight is very precious." 1 Peter 3:4, R.S.V. Finally, he begged them to preserve "unity of spirit, sympathy, love of the brethren, a tender heart and a humble mind." 1 Peter 3:8, R.S.V.

Thus he preached love. Pure, selfless love.

So did John. "Little children," he wrote, "let us not love in word or speech but in deed and in truth." 1 John 3:18, R.S.V.

"Beloved," he said, "let us love one another; for love is of God, and he who loves is born of God and knows God. He who does not love does not know God; for God is love." 1 John 4:7, 8, R.S.V.

Paul's epistles are likewise filled with the same radiant message. They are love letters in the noblest sense.

"If I speak in the tongues of men and of angels, but have not love," he told the Corinthians, "I am a noisy gong or a clanging cymbal.

"And if I have prophetic powers, and understand

all mysteries and all knowledge, and if I have all faith, so as to remove mountains, but have not love, I am nothing.

"If I give away all I have, and if I deliver my body to be burned, but have not love, I gain nothing." 1 Corinthians 13:1-3, R.S.V.

Then he went on to describe true love and how it reveals itself.

" Love is patient and kind," he said; "love is not jealous or boastful; it is not arrogant or rude.

"Love does not insist on its own way; it is not irritable or resentful; it does not rejoice at wrong, but rejoices in the right.

"Love bears all things, believes all things, hopes all things, endures all things.

"Love never ends; as for prophecy, it will pass away; as for tongues, they will cease; as for knowledge, it will pass away. . . .

"So faith, hope, love abide, these three; but the greatest of these is love." Verses 4-13, R.S.V.

Then he added, "Make love your aim," a wonderful objective for every man, woman, and child, both then and now. 1 Corinthians 14:1, R.S.V.

He wanted everybody, inside the church and out of it, to be thus motivated. Not by silly sentiment, but by true love. Love that is patient and kind. Love that keeps people from being jealous, boastful, proud, or rude. Love that bears hardship without complaint, believes the best about others, is always full of hope, and endures suffering with a smile.

This is love at its best. It is the love that led Jesus to

the cross; the love that flows from that cross like a glowing river of fire, consuming every kind of selfishness and replacing it with the sweet and lovely traits of Christ's own beautiful character.

This is the sort of love Paul prayed for when he wrote to the Ephesians: "I bow my knees before the Father, from whom every family in heaven and on earth is named, that according to the riches of His glory He may grant you to be strengthened with might through His Spirit in the inner man, and that Christ may dwell in your hearts through faith; that you, being *rooted and grounded in love,* may have power to comprehend with all the saints what is the breadth and length and height and depth, and to *know the love of Christ* which surpasses knowledge, that you may be filled with all the fullness of God." Ephesians 3:14-19, R.S.V.

It was a beautiful prayer, redolent with the fragrance of heaven. He desired only that the Holy Spirit should so fill their hearts with love that, besides being "rooted and grounded in love," their capacity to love would expand continuously without limit, in length and breadth and height and depth, even as the love of Christ is immeasurable.

When writing to the new Christians in Colossae, he expressed the special desire that they should be "knit together in love." Colossians 2:2, R.S.V.

The original word used here has the thought of *bringing together,* as when one knots two pieces of string, or knits two pieces of wool, or welds two pieces of iron.

And that is exactly what true love does. It brings people together, and keeps them together. Families. Friends. Church members. It knits them so closely that separation and divorce become impossible.

Farther on in this letter Paul pleaded with the people to *put off* such unlovely things as "anger, wrath, malice, slander, and foul talk," and *put on* "compassion, kindness, lowliness, meekness, and patience, forbearing one another and . . . forgiving each other." Then he added: "And above all these *put on love,* which binds everything together in perfect harmony." Colossians 3:8, 12-14, R.S.V.

Glorious indeed was his concept of the power of love. And it was this, above all else, that gave the Christian church such impetus that it spread like a prairie fire, sweeping on and on across the then-known world, consuming pagan temples, pagan idols, even the pagan philosophy of life.

Christ said that He would set the world on fire, and He did. And this fire will never go out. It is still burning. And it will continue to burn till His wondrous purpose is achieved.

Courage then! If your heart is full of the love of God, you have nothing to fear for the future, no matter how dark and sinister it may prove to be. For love "abides." Love prevails.

Its victory is assured and inevitable.

It cannot fail.

It is a fire unquenchable.

The loveless, the heartless, the cruel, will fade at last into "outer darkness," but those with true love in their hearts will glow with ever-growing brilliance not only amid the gathering storm, but on and on through all eternity. Their warm, helpful, cheerful radiance will never grow dim. The fire within them will never go out. They will "shine as the brightness of the firmament; and . . . as the stars forever and ever." Daniel 12:3.

14

TRIUMPHANT FAITH

*I*T IS strange but true that while love begets love it also incites hatred. Often those who don't want to be loved develop a fierce and unreasoning antagonism against those who try to love them.

This is the basic cause of most persecutions and much of man's inhumanity to man. Loveless souls, resenting the gentle, pious lives of the true followers of Jesus, seek to rid themselves of this constant rebuke of their evil ways.

The early Christians ran into this sort of opposition continually. But they were not surprised. Jesus warned them ahead of time.

"Be on your guard," He had said. "You will be handed over to the courts. You will be flogged in synagogues. You will be summoned to appear before governors and kings on My account. . . . Do not worry. . . . Brother will betray brother to death, and the father his child; children will turn against their parents and send them to their death. All will hate you for your allegiance to Me; but the man who holds out to the end will be saved." Mark 13: 9-13, N.E.B.

"If the world hates you," He had said to them on another occasion, "it hated Me first, as you know well. If you belonged to the world, the world would love its own; but because you do not belong to the world, because I have chosen you out of the world, for that reason the world hates you. . . . As they persecuted Me, they will persecute you." John 15:18-20, N.E.B.

The Master's words came true almost immediately. Right after Pentecost, Peter ran into trouble in the temple, as we have already seen. Then Stephen was stoned to death.

"At that time," says the record, "there was a great persecution against the church which was at Jerusalem; and they were all scattered abroad throughout the regions of Judea and Samaria, except the apostles." Acts 8:1.

But the apostles didn't escape for long, for King Herod "stretched forth his hands to vex certain of the church. And he killed James the brother of John with the sword." Acts 12:1, 2. Then he arrested Peter.

One of the worst troublemakers at that time was a man called Saul, a member of the Sanhedrin, who was forever "breathing out threatenings and slaughter against the disciples of the Lord." Acts 9:1. He hated the church so much that Jesus had to deal with him personally.

"Saul, Saul, why do you persecute Me?" He asked on the Damascus road.

The result was another convert to the gospel. Saul the persecutor became Paul the apostle. Then *he* learned what it means to be persecuted.

Enraged because he had changed sides, his old friends turned upon him in fury. He became the most wanted Christian convert, escaping from Damascus only by descending the city wall in a basket. Jerusalem proved equally inhospitable, and from there he fled to his home town of Tarsus. Thereafter trouble dogged his footsteps the rest of his days.

"I will show him how great things he must suffer for My name's sake," said Jesus (Acts 9:16), and never was a truer word spoken.

At Lystra, Paul was stoned so severely that onlookers thought he was dead. Acts 14:19. At Philippi he was sorely beaten and then imprisoned. Acts 16:23. At Ephesus "the whole city was filled with confusion" because of his witness, and once more he had to flee for his life. Acts 19:29.

Proclaiming the love of God in Christ was no easy task in those far-off years. While some received the message with gladness, others bitterly opposed it.

The cause of all the trouble was that love was turning the world "upside down" (Acts 17:6), and the world didn't want to be disturbed. It preferred its old, cruel, wicked ways, which true love would destroy. So it persecuted, fighting viciously for survival.

What started out as a simple presentation of the love of God in Christ became a struggle, a battle, a war, with Christians identified by the love they bore for each other, and their enemies by the hatred in their hearts for the name of Christ.

It took courage to be a Christian then.

Nor did the situation improve with the passing years. Persecution grew worse. As pagan priests and merchants saw their vested interests jeopardized they joined in the hue and cry against the new religion. Acts 19:24-28. As Roman authorities saw—or thought they saw—the security of the state threatened by people who exalted their Leader above Caesar they raised the cry of "Treason!" with all its dreadful penalties.

Terrible became the sufferings of the Christians then. They were imprisoned, tortured, crucified, thrown to the lions, and burned at the stake. Like the martyrs of an earlier era they faced "jeers and flogging, even fetters and prison bars. They were stoned, they were sawn in two, they were put to the sword, they went about dressed in skins of sheep or goats, in poverty, distress, and misery. They were too good for this world." Hebrews 11:36-38, N.E.B.

During the ten-year Diocletian persecution (A.D. 303-313), the church was almost wiped out. When the pressure eased at last, 318 of the bishops who remained met at the Council of Nicea in A.D. 325. Some were blind and others crippled. Almost all bore some evidence of sufferings endured.

Under Constantine the Great came peace, tolerance, and expansion. But as centuries passed prosperity brought apostasy; so much so that when at last the church took over the empire and its leader sat on the throne of the Caesars, it became a worse persecutor than the pagans it had dispossessed.

Now the true people of God literally went underground as they sought refuge in caves, catacombs, mountain fastnesses, and poverty-stricken homes in order to preserve their faith. Even so they were hunted like wild beasts and, when caught, treated with shocking barbarity.

When the light of truth was fanned to new flame by Wycliffe, Huss, Luther, Zwingli, Knox, and other Reformers, the organization that falsely claimed to be the church reacted with great violence, making no pretense of exhibiting the spirit of Christ. With dragon-like ferocity it sought to stamp out what it termed "heresy," and for no other reason than that its vested interests were threatened. The so-called "Holy Office" of the Inquisition, inaugurated at the beginning of the thirteenth century to crush the last remnants of resistance among the Albigenses, was given increased powers, and tens of thousands of suspected heretics were tortured and killed at its instigation. In Spain, Portugal, Italy, and Poland the Reformation was almost totally crushed by fire and sword. In France it was likewise well-nigh obliterated. According to the historian Llorente over thirty thousand persons were burned alive in Spain and more than two hundred thousand "penitents" were forced into submission "by

water, weights, fire, pulleys, and screws" and "all the
apparatus by which the sinews could be strained without cracking, the bones bruised without breaking, the
body racked exquisitely without giving up the ghost."

Century after century the terror continued until,
to use one historian's graphic description, almost all
Europe had been turned into "a slaughterhouse, a
charnel house, an Akeldama."

In 1655 John Milton wrote his famous poem concerning the horrible massacre of the Waldenses by Charles
Emmanuel II, Duke of Savoy:

> Avenge, O Lord, Thy slaughtered saints, whose bones
>   Lie scattered on the Alpine mountains cold;
>   Even them who kept Thy truth so pure of old,
> When all our fathers worshiped stocks and stones,
> Forget not: in Thy book record their groans
>   Who were Thy sheep, and in their ancient fold
>   Slain by the bloody Piemontese, that rolled
> Mother with infant down the rocks. Their moans
> The vales redoubled to the hills, and they
>   To heaven.

What courage it must have taken to be a Christian
in those days!

When at last the Reformation prevailed, persecution, at least in its more violent forms, declined. Yet
even today, nearly twenty centuries after Calvary,
there are many lands where it is still dangerous to be
a true disciple of Jesus. In recent years, behind the
iron curtain, the bamboo curtain, and where clerical
tyranny still holds sway, thousands have suffered
imprisonment, torture, confiscation of property, and

death because of their witness for the gospel of Jesus.

It takes courage to be a true Christian now!

Looking back over the whole tragic story one wonders how even a remnant of the church survived. The opposition was always so strong, so cruel, so filled with acrimonious hatred. Yet always, even in the worst of times, there were a few who preserved the precious teachings of Jesus, no matter what the cost to themselves.

The infant church was almost crushed, at the outset, by the unbelieving Jews, led by Saul of Tarsus; it was well-nigh wiped out by Roman emperors such as Diocletian and Galerius; it was brought to the verge of extinction by the papal persecutions of the Dark Ages; yet, miraculously, it outlasted all its foes.

Why? What was it that enabled simple, ordinary men and women to endure so much, to hold out so long against such frightful odds, and—most wonderful of all—to pass on their faith to their children?

It was heroic, resolute, triumphant faith. It was noble, dauntless, unwavering courage; courage drawn from the cross, that symbol of suffering love.

Remembering what Christ had done for them, their own trials seemed but a light affliction.

Recalling that God so loved the world that He went to Calvary for them, they were willing to go there, too, for Him.

Like true lovers, they were ready to be loyal to their Beloved whatever the price might be.

When darkness deepened, and terrors threatened, they remembered the reassuring words of Jesus, "Fear not, little flock; for it is your Father's good pleasure to give you the kingdom." Luke 12:32.

They recalled His beautiful promise to the church at Smyrna: "Be thou faithful unto death, and I will give thee a crown of life." Revelation 2:10.

They thought, too, of Peter's precious counsel, made tenfold more significant because he, too, died a martyr's death, crucified upside down: "If you should suffer, . . . count yourselves happy. Have no fear: . . . do not be perturbed, but hold the Lord Christ in reverence in your hearts." 1 Peter 3:14, 15, N.E.B.

Sometimes, perhaps, they imagined they could hear the dear old fisherman saying in his simple, kindly way, "My dear friends, do not be bewildered by the fiery ordeal that is upon you, as though it were something extraordinary. It gives you a share in Christ's sufferings, and that is cause for joy; and when His glory is revealed, your joy will be triumphant." 1 Peter 4:12-14. N.E.B.

Thus sustained, the martyrs went to their death with amazing gallantry, always thinking of others rather than themselves.

"Lord, open the king of England's eyes!" cried William Tyndale, famous translator of the Bible, as he awaited his cruel fate.

"How long, O God! shall darkness cover this kingdom? How long wilt Thou suffer this tyranny of men?" cried Patrick Hamilton of St. Andrews, Scotland, as he endured excruciating agonies in a slow, smoldering fire.

"Be of good comfort, Master Ridley, and play the man," called Dr. Latimer to his fellow sufferer at the stake in Oxford, as smoke and flames rose around them. "We shall this day light such a candle, by God's grace, in England, as I trust shall never be put out."

So throughout seemingly unendurable hardships courage flowed into the hearts of these faithful witnesses for Christ and thousands of others like them. Wonderful courage. Courage sufficient for their most awful needs.

Today, as the final storm gathers, and the powers of darkness make ready anew to "wage war . . . on those who keep God's commandments and maintain their testimony to Jesus" (Revelation 12:17, N.E.B.), we shall need similar courage to endure. Fortunate indeed will be those who know how and where to find it.

15

GLORY
OF CALVARY

BECAUSE the death of Christ on the cross was the ultimate sacrifice, the ultimate in suffering, significance, and sublimity of purpose, the stream of courage flowing from it is timelessly and universally efficacious.

Concerning the unique *suffering* involved, Bishop Westcott, the great Bible commentator, wrote: "Man as he is cannot feel the full significance of death, . . . but Christ in His sinlessness perfectly realized its awfulness. In this fact lies the immeasurable difference between the death of Christ, simply as death, and that of the holiest martyr." In other words, the fearful penalty for sin fell with peculiarly awful impact upon the

As Jesus rode into Jerusalem to die on Calvary's cross the grace of God "dawned upon the world with healing for all mankind." Blessings innumerable stem from His sacrifice, with courage and hope for every crisis.

143

One who possessed all the delicate sensitiveness of a perfect character, to whom sin was utterly repugnant and whose mind was completely in tune with that of His holy Father.

Concerning the unique *significance* of the cross, Dr. A. C. Dixon, famous preacher of the Old Metropolitan Tabernacle in London, wrote: "Put all into one . . . all Truth, all Light, all Life, all Wisdom, all Power, all Holiness, all Love incarnate in one Man, who gives Himself for the untruthful, for the darkened, for the dead, for the weak, for the unholy, for the unlovely,— and you have some conception of what the cross of Jesus Christ is in its deeper meaning."—*The Glories of the Cross,* pages 12, 13.

Concerning the unique *sublimity of purpose* involved, the apostle Paul had this to say: "The divine nature was His from the first; yet He did not think to snatch at equality with God, but made Himself nothing, assuming the nature of a slave. Bearing the human likeness, revealed in human shape, He humbled Himself, and in obedience accepted even death—death on a cross." Philippians 2:6-9, N.E.B.

Again, in his epistle to Titus he wrote: "The grace of God has dawned upon the world with healing for all mankind; and by it we are disciplined to renounce godless ways and worldly desires, and to live a life of temperance, honesty, and godliness in the present age, looking forward to the happy fulfillment of our hopes when the splendor of our great God and Saviour Christ Jesus will appear. He it is who sacrificed Himself for us, to set us free from all wickedness and to make us a pure people marked out for His own, eager to do good." Titus 2:11-14, N.E.B.

Because of all this—of what it cost, of what it meant, and of the majestic purpose behind it—the cross is incomparable as a source of spiritual fortitude. Not only does the thought of it sustain the heart in times of great trial and persecution but also in all the lesser but very real perplexities of everyday living. Offering as it does perpetual evidence of God's love and of His desire and purpose to love us to the uttermost, it removes every cause for anxiety and provides escape from every temptation.

To one and all it says: "God is faithful, and He will not let you be tempted beyond your strength, but with the temptation will also provide the way of escape, that you may be able to endure it." 1 Corinthians 10:13, R.S.V.

If we are tempted to worry about temporal necessities it says: "If God is on our side, who is against us? He did not spare His own Son, but surrendered Him for us all; and with this gift how can He fail to lavish upon us all He has to give?" Romans 8:31, 32, N.E.B.

The cross did but confirm the Master's beautiful assurance to His disciples: "If God so clothes the grass of the field, which today is alive and tomorrow is thrown into the oven, will He not much more clothe you, O men of little faith? Therefore do not be anxious, saying, 'What shall we eat?' or 'What shall we drink?' or 'What shall we wear?' For the Gentiles seek all these things; and your heavenly Father knows that you need them all. But seek first His kingdom and His righteousness, and all these things shall be yours as well." Matthew 6:30-33, R.S.V.

If we are tempted to lose heart because of past mistakes and failures the cross, with arms pointing in opposite directions, cries out to us, "As far as the east is from the west, so far hath He removed our transgressions from us." Psalm 103:12.

How far is that? Nobody knows. Nobody ever will know. It is an infinite distance. The phrase is but one of God's glorious superlatives to indicate the greatness of His forgiving mercy.

Akin to it is His forthright declaration: "Though your sins be as scarlet, they shall be as white as snow; though they be red like crimson, they shall be as wool." Isaiah 1:18.

This calls for a miracle, but God is well able to perform it. As the prophet Micah said: "Who is a God like Thee, pardoning iniquity and passing over transgression for the remnant of His inheritance? He does not retain His anger forever because He delights in steadfast love. He will again have compassion upon us, He will tread our iniquities underfoot. Thou wilt cast all our sins into the depths of the sea." Micah 7:18, 19, R.S.V.

When Micah wrote those words he didn't know how deep the sea was. Nobody did until a few years ago. Nobody, that is, except God. All along He knew that in some places the bottom is more than seven miles down, where the pressure is several tons to the square inch. And there, He says, He will cast all our confessed and forgiven sins—down where they can never be found and where we never need worry about them any more.

If we are tempted to yield to great pressures or strong allurements, we should remember that He who died on the cross was "made like His brethren in every respect, so that He might become a merciful and faithful High Priest in the service of God, to make expiation for the sins of the people. For because He Himself has suffered and been tempted, He is able to help those who are tempted." Hebrews 2:17, 18, R.S.V.

Consequently, "we have not a high priest who is unable to sympathize with our weaknesses, but one who in every respect has been tempted as we are, yet without sinning. Let us then with confidence draw near to the throne of grace, that we may receive mercy and find grace to help in time of need." Hebrews 4: 15, 16, R.S.V.

This help will be forthcoming at the right moment, at the right place, just when we need it most. For not only is Jesus "able to keep" us from falling (Jude 24); He is "able also to save them to the uttermost that come unto God by Him, seeing He ever liveth to make intercession for them." Hebrews 7:25.

If we are tempted to feel unwanted and lonely, the voice from the cross will have this message of consolation for us: "If a man loves Me, he will keep My word, and My Father will love him, and We will come to him and make Our home with him." John 14:23, R.S.V.

This amazing desire for perpetual fellowship with all who love Him is again revealed in the Master's beautiful prayer recorded in John 17: "Neither pray I for these alone, but for them also which shall believe on Me through their word; that they all may be one; as Thou, Father, art in Me, and I in Thee, that they also may be one in Us." Verses 20, 21.

With this same most gracious purpose in mind He says to us, as He did to His disciples of old, "Lo, I am with you alway, even unto the end of the world." Matthew 28:20.

If we are tempted to feel insecure and doubtful, we can take heart from this wonderful assurance: "My sheep hear My voice, and I know them, and they follow Me; and I give them eternal life, and they shall never perish, and no one shall snatch them out of My hand." John 10:27, 28, R.S.V.

We shall be safe in the hand of the Lord of love so long as we want to stay there. Nor is separation even *possible* if we desire to remain in full fellowship with Him. As Paul says in one of the greatest passages in all his writings: "Who shall separate us from the love of Christ? Shall tribulation, or distress, or persecution, or famine, or nakedness, or peril, or sword? . . . No, in all these things we are more than conquerors through Him who loved us. For I am sure that neither death, nor life, nor angels, nor principalities, nor things present, nor things to come, nor powers, nor height, nor depth, nor anything else in all creation, will be able to separate us from the love of God in Christ Jesus our Lord." Romans 8:35-39, R.S.V.

If we are tempted to feel "left out" or discriminated against, for any reason at all, we should listen to this glorious declaration: "Whosoever believeth on Him shall not be ashamed. For there is no difference between the Jew and the Greek: for the same Lord over all is rich unto all that call upon Him. For whosoever shall call upon the name of the Lord shall be saved." Romans 10:11-13.

That word "whosoever" may be somewhat obsolete nowadays, but it is one of the most precious in the King James Version of the Bible. It is so all-inclusive, taking in everybody, leaving no one out. It appears also in John 3:16, where Jesus tells us that "God so loved, . . . that *whosoever* believeth in Him should not perish, but have everlasting life." It occurs again in His final invitation found in Revelation 22:17: "And the Spirit and the bride say, Come. And let him that heareth say, Come. And let him that is athirst come. And *whosoever* will, let him take the water of life freely."

Later versions have substituted the less picturesque "all" or "everyone" in these passages, but the meaning is the same. There is no discrimination with God. His arms encircle everybody. His heart of love is big enough to take in young and old, rich and poor, high and low, of "every nation, and kindred, and tongue, and people." Revelation 14:6.

If we are tempted to give up hope, perhaps through overwork, disappointment, or the hardness of the way, the voice from the cross says: "Come unto Me, all ye that labor and are heavy-laden, and I will give you rest. Take My yoke upon you, and learn of Me; for I am meek and lowly in heart: and ye shall find rest unto your souls." Matthew 11:28, 29.

Again, "Because you have kept My word of patient endurance, I will keep you from the hour of trial which is coming on the whole world, to try those who dwell upon the earth. I am coming soon; hold fast what you have, so that no one may seize your crown." Revelation 3:10, 11, R.S.V.

Herein we glimpse anew the shining glory of the cross, whereby God has provided for every possible situation which might wear down our morale, weaken our resistance to evil, or lessen the effectiveness of our witness for truth and right. Its radiance reaches around the globe, to all men everywhere, in their most urgent and desperate needs.

"I, if I be lifted up from the earth," said Jesus, "will draw all men unto Me." John 12:32. That is what He has been doing down the centuries, ever since Calvary. That is what He is doing now. Drawing men to Him, like a mighty magnet. Drawing you, drawing me, drawing everybody. Offering pardon, fellowship, and peace. Offering strength for today and hope for tomorrow.

To all who accept His offer He promises ample courage for any crisis, saying, "I will not fail you or forsake you." Joshua 1:5, R.S.V.

Part Four

COURAGE FROM GOOD HABITS

Reading the Bible, either alone or in family worship, is one of the best and most rewarding of all good habits; for God speaks through this Book, giving help and blessing in every time of need.

KEN GUNALL, ARTIST

© P.P.P.A.

16

STRENGTH FROM MEDITATION

OVER forty years ago I attended a Baptist church in England to hear a sermon by Dr. F. B. Meyer, at that time renowned for his great preaching on both sides of the Atlantic. However, instead of giving a profound, sparkling discourse such as I had expected, he presented a simple Bible study. I came away disappointed and disillusioned. It took me years to learn that it was the very simplicity of that study which made it so truly powerful, so lastingly helpful.

Even now, four decades and two world wars later, I remember the theme as well as if I had heard it last night. It was: "Keep Up the Good Old Habits."

I recall how the preacher said that no matter what might happen to us in the future, no matter how discouraged we might become, we should never stop reading the Bible, saying our prayers, keeping the Sabbath, and going to church. Just keeping up these good old habits would, sooner or later, bring hope and cheer to our hearts again.

How right he was!

All too often, when we get "down" or "blue," we use our depression as an excuse for staying home from church, failing to say our prayers, and passing up Bible study. Yet how foolish to cut ourselves off from these precious sources of courage just when we need them most!

Consider Bible reading for a few moments and see what a blessing it can be to us.

I am aware, of course, that many people regard Bible reading as a terrible bore. They say the Book is too dry, too stuffy, too out of date. It isn't, really. Wisely read and rightly understood, it is the most fascinating Book ever written, with a story and a plot more thrilling than any offered today in the most exciting novels.

Reading the Bible—the right way—is perhaps the most rewarding of all occupations. There is so much in it of lasting value, so much accumulated wisdom of the ages, so much help in understanding life. Herein, as we have already seen, is the most marvelous revelation of God's love to man, with all that this can mean to us in strength for today and hope for tomorrow.

Some people, unfortunately, don't know how to read

the Bible. They follow the hop, skip, and jump method, turning at random from one passage to another, hoping to find something of interest. This is very superficial and will never provide a true picture of the Bible and its over-all purpose and message.

Others start at the beginning, determined to read on to the end whether they understand it or not. Such usually give up in despair before they have finished Leviticus or Deuteronomy. Even if they struggle gallantly through these earlier books they bog down permanently when they get to Ezekiel, Daniel, or the minor prophets.

There is a better way. Here are a few suggestions:

1. Begin with one of the simplest books, such as the Gospel of Mark. Read it through. It won't take long, not more than an hour at the most.

Here is the earliest record of the life and death of Jesus Christ, as told by eyewitnesses to John Mark. The many references to Peter suggest that much of the information was provided by the big fisherman himself, which makes the story even more interesting.

Mark's Gospel is full of action, and you will find it very easy reading. It will introduce you not only to the New Testament but also to the basic facts of the Christian faith.

2. Next read the Gospel of Matthew. This book was written several years later than Mark's and repeats almost every line of it. In addition, however, it gives many of the teachings of Jesus that Mark omitted.

Matthew reports six of the sermons of Jesus, the first and most familiar being the Sermon on the Mount.

In this are found the Beatitudes, the golden rule, and the Lord's Prayer.

3. Next read the Gospel written by Luke, whose obvious interest in medical matters gave him a humanitarian outlook and led him to record the parables of the good Samaritan, the prodigal son, and the rich man and Lazarus.

4. Now read the Gospel of John, which was written at least thirty years after the other three. During this time the Christian church had become established, and John was led to record for its encouragement his most treasured memories of Jesus.

When you have read the four Gospels you will have had the finest possible introduction to the Bible. You will be prepared to go forward to the book of Acts to read Luke's story of the growth of the early church; or, if you prefer, turn back to Genesis to find the beginning of the tragedy of sin, which ultimately caused Christ's death.

5. Look for the stories in the Bible. There are hundreds. If you happen to possess the ten-volume set of *The Bible Story* you will find 409 stories listed in the index.

In searching for all these stories and retelling them in language simple enough for children to understand, I learned more about the Bible than I had ever known before. I found it to be the most fascinating book I had ever read. You can make the same discovery.

6. Pick out the biographies. The Bible is full of them. Unlike many books of biography, it tells the bad as well as the good points of its various characters.

You could concentrate first on Joseph and read all that is said about him from his birth as Rachel's first-born to the proud day when Pharaoh placed the destiny of Egypt in his hands. See Genesis 37 to 50 for his life story.

Then study Moses, the great emancipator of the Hebrews, and follow his amazing course from the day his mother placed him in an ark of bulrushes by the river Nile till he stood on Mount Sinai and talked with God "face to face." Exodus 1 to 22, 24, 31 to 35, and Numbers 10 to 27 will bring you the high lights of his story.

Joshua will give you many thrilling moments, from the time he won Israel's first battle with the Amalekites (Exodus 17:9-13) through to the capture of Jericho, Ai, and finally all Palestine. See the book of Joshua.

David, of course, you will enjoy. From the moment he steps on the Bible stage as an innocent shepherd lad to his last stirring oration as the dying king of Israel, his story will grip your heart. Incidentally, his is the longest biography in the Old Testament, covering about one thirteenth of the whole. You will find most of it in 1 Samuel, chapters 16 to 31, all of 2 Samuel, and the first and second chapters of 1 Kings.

In the New Testament the most notable biography, apart from the story of Jesus and occasional glimpses of His disciples, is that of Paul. He steps on the scene in Acts 7:58 as an official of the Sanhedrin at the stoning of Stephen, moves to the center of the stage in chapter 9, and stays there through most of the remainder of the book. His three missionary journeys are described in much detail as he strives to bring the story of Christ to Jerusalem, Damascus, Antioch, Tarsus, Athens, Corinth, Philippi, Ephesus, and finally to Rome. He was the great city evangelist of the first century A.D., with a story you should not fail to read.

7. Another highly profitable approach to the Bible is to look upon it as a library in which to pursue a variety of studies. For this purpose a good concordance is necessary. Also very helpful is a reference Bible.

With these valuable aids you can choose any one of hundreds of subjects and find out what the Bible has to say about it.

You may perhaps decide to study the subject of Faith. What is it? How does God value it, and why? How important is it in the Christian life? The Bible will answer all such vital questions.

Obedience and Disobedience is another intriguing subject, also Love and Hatred, Faithfulness and Unfaithfulness, Greed and Liberality, Justice and Injustice, Joy and Sorrow.

You will want to look into the Mercy of God and His Judgments, the Importance of Law and Grace, and the Rewards of the Righteous and the Wicked.

Another fascinating study is Prophecy. The Bible is full of it, as noted in previous chapters. All manner of predictions are on record, with their fulfillment. Nothing will increase your confidence in the Bible so much as the discovery that the forecasts of its prophets have unfailingly come to pass.

But don't try to read too much at once. Don't set yourself so many chapters or passages to read by a certain time. Take it easy. Relax. Bible reading is not a race or an endurance trial. Nor is there any special virtue in reading it through in so many hours, days, or weeks. Its rich treasures are not extracted by high-speed, high-pressure methods. Rapid scanning won't help you very much. Read it slowly, thoughtfully, prayerfully.

The Bible is a book for meditation. Far better read one chapter slowly, thoughtfully, prayerfully, than a whole book in a wild hurry to reach the last verse or accomplish some predetermined program.

Take time to enjoy it. Try to think what the words really mean. Roll the lovely phrases around in your mind. You will be surprised how beautiful they will become.

Frequently I have spent hours of concentrated thought on a few brief verses, and how very rewarding it has always been! This is when the Bible positively glows. When at length you put it down you have a feeling that you have been in the very presence of God.

Glorious thoughts come leaping up from seemingly dry and meaningless words, like snowdrops bursting from the barren earth in the spring. Passages to which you have never before given much attention become like harp strings upon which angels play the melodies of heaven.

When writing *The Bible Story* I had this experience many times.

This is how it happens:

Take, for instance, the following passage from the Gospel of Luke: "And it came to pass the day after, that He went into a city called Nain; and many of His disciples went with Him, and much people. Now when He came nigh to the gate of the city, behold, there was a dead man carried out, the only son of his mother, and she was a widow: and much people of the city was with her. And when the Lord saw her, He had compassion on her, and said unto her, Weep not. And He came and touched the bier: and they that bare him stood still. And He said, Young man, I say unto thee, Arise. And he that was dead sat up, and began to speak. And He delivered him to his mother." Luke 7:11-15.

At first glance this is merely the record of a kind deed done for a poor widow. By tradition it is known as the Raising of the Widow's Son. But if you stop to think about it a little while, it becomes truly radiant with loveliness and power.

Suddenly you see two processions, not one. The first is made up of Jesus and His disciples; the second of the poor widow and the mourners. One is moving into the city of Nain, the other out of it. One is led by the Prince of life, the other by a corpse. One is a procession of joy, the other of sorrow. Suddenly they both meet, and life triumphs over death. This is why I call the story, "The Interrupted Funeral," for that is exactly what it was. That is what Jesus came to do—to make funerals forever obsolete by giving everlasting life to all who will accept it. His resurrection ensures the resurrection of all the saints, and will banish death for all eternity.

Take a look now at this passage from Luke 23:50-53:

"And, behold, there was a man named Joseph, a counselor; and he was a good man, and a just: (the same had not consented to the counsel and deed of them;) he was of Arimathea, a city of the Jews: who also himself waited for the kingdom of God. This man went unto Pilate, and begged the body of Jesus. And he took it down, and wrapped it in linen, and laid it in a sepulcher that was hewn in stone, wherein never man before was laid."

As one reads this for the first time it appears to be just a brief report of what happened to the body of Jesus immediately after the crucifixion. But stop a moment. Don't rush by so fast! Read it again. Then again. Compare it with John 19:38-40 and watch it begin to glow.

See! A ladder has been placed against the cross. An old man is climbing it, while another waits anxiously below. Now the man on the ladder is drawing out the nails that hold Jesus to the cross. But he needs help. Another ladder is raised. The second old man climbs it. Then together, very gently, they lower the body to the ground, perhaps with the limp arms of the Master around their necks as though He were saying to them, "Thank you, friends, for coming; thank you for helping Me." What a beautiful thought it is that when His own special friends had forsaken Him and fled, these two old men, "secret disciples," came to His aid! Even more thrilling is the sudden realization that though someone who hated Jesus drove in the nails, someone who loved Him pulled them out!

Still another illustration of the value of quietly

163

meditating upon the Bible may be found in the story recorded in John 21:9-13:

"As soon then as they were come to land, they saw a fire of coals there, and fish laid thereon, and bread. Jesus saith unto them, Bring of the fish which ye have now caught. Simon Peter went up, and drew the net to land full of great fishes, an hundred and fifty and three: and for all there were so many, yet was not the net broken. Jesus saith unto them, Come and dine. And none of the disciples durst ask Him, Who art Thou? knowing that it was the Lord. Jesus then cometh, and taketh bread, and giveth them, and fish likewise."

At first glance this appears to be simply an account of Jesus' last meeting with His disciples by Galilee. Further study, however, will reveal that it is a mine of spiritual blessing.

Note the "fire of coals." Who lighted it? Jesus, of course. Not for Himself, but for His cold, weary disciples who had toiled all night and had caught nothing. And He had "fish laid thereon." How kind and thoughtful of Him to provide them with food at such an early hour! And then He said, "Come and dine," or rather, as we would say today, "Come and have breakfast."

Beautiful, unforgettable scene! Jesus, the Lord of life, just risen from the dead, asking His earthly friends to breakfast with Him! Surely this is one of the sweetest invitations in all the Bible. As breakfast is the first meal of the day, so that meal marked the beginning of a new day and a new life for the disciples. Fishing on Galilee for them was over forever. From now on they were to go forth in their Master's name and catch men for the kingdom of God.

These few examples, taken at random, show how anybody—just anybody—can find the most delightfully inspiring thoughts in the Bible. Here, perhaps, is the most convincing proof of its inspiration. It inspires those who read it. It stimulates the mind, uplifts the thoughts, and sets the heart aglow.

This is why you should not only make a habit of reading the Bible but *keep up the habit,* no matter what happens. Read it regularly, whether you are riding "the high places of the earth," or walking in the valley of shadows. It will never disappoint you. Unfailingly it will bring you help in "every time of need." Hebrews 4:16.

No matter which version you may possess—whether it be the King James, the Revised Standard, the New English, or Weymouth's, Moffatt's, Goodspeed's, Knox's, or Phillips's, God will speak to you through the precious words enshrined therein.

He will speak to you of faith, hope, and love, and will bring you strength and courage sufficient for the worst crises you will ever face.

17

POWER FROM COMMUNION

PRAYER is another of the "good old habits" we must preserve if we would keep up our courage. Come good days or bad, we must keep on praying in faith.

Not merely *saying* prayers. Too often that becomes nothing more than muttering "vain repitition." To be effective, prayer must come from the heart and reach up by faith to God.

The person who knows how to pray holds the key to the treasury of heaven. He can have anything he needs.

Breath-taking are the divine promises to those whose lives are pleasing to God, who love to walk and talk with Him day by day.

Think of this, for instance: "No good thing will He withhold from them that walk uprightly." Psalm 84:11.

And this: "They that seek the Lord shall not want any good thing." Psalm 34:10.

And this: "Delight thyself also in the Lord; and He shall give thee the desires of thine heart." Psalm 37:4.

"The Lord shall open unto thee His good treasure," Moses told the children of Israel (Deuteronomy 28:12), which was like saying, "If there is anything you want, come and take it."

Nor was this promise restricted to the children of Abraham. God is no respecter of persons. He is equally generous to all who love and obey Him, in every generation.

To His disciples Jesus said, "If you ask anything in My name I will do it." John 14:14, N.E.B. Again, "If you dwell in Me, and My words dwell in you, ask what you will, and you shall have it." John 15:7, N.E.B.

If we choose to be His disciples these promises are for us. What could be more magnanimous? They read like a blank check on the bank of heaven.

If words mean anything, God has made provision for every holy desire of ours to be granted. If we are anxious, fearful, discouraged, it is not because He wills it so. If we are weak, wretched, and spiritually impoverished the fault is ours, not His. He has planned greatly for us. He stands ready to be very gracious to us, to fill our lives with blessings and make us strong enough to cope with every emergency. If we "have not" it is because we "ask not." James 4:2.

One reason why Jesus came to this earth and died

on Calvary's cross was to enrich our lives in every possible way. "You know how generous our Lord Jesus Christ has been," wrote the apostle Paul. "He was rich, yet for your sake He became poor, so that through His poverty you might become rich." 2 Corinthians 8:9, N.E.B.

Not rich necessarily in material things, for these count but little in the sight of God, but rich in the things of the Spirit, which alone have lasting value. Through Him we can become rich in wisdom, knowledge, faith, love—and courage!

"If any of you falls short in wisdom," wrote James, "he should ask God for it and it will be given him, for God is a generous giver who neither refuses nor reproaches anyone." James 1:5, N.E.B.

God's generosity is so limitless that it covers every conceivable need we may have. If we lack wisdom, or faith, or courage, or anything else, we are to make our need known to Him and He will supply it. If as we eye the gathering storm we feel nervous and afraid, we are to tell Him of our weakness and He will replace it with strength sufficient to meet the crisis valiantly.

We should not hesitate to talk to Him and tell Him all that is on our hearts. When He says, "Come now, and let us reason together" (Isaiah 1:18), He has in mind much more than a discussion of our sins. He is interested in everything about us, the big things as well as the little things.

Some people's prayers give the impression that God is only concerned with trivial matters. They request fine weather at a school picnic, or that Johnny may get good grades in an exam, or that Mary may meet her boy friend on time. While it is good to believe that God is concerned with all the details of our lives, we should never be reticent in mentioning to Him the heavier burdens we are carrying or the deeper desires of our hearts. He wants us to bring these larger matters to Him. It is His special joy to do great things for His children, for He "is able to do exceeding abundantly above all that we ask or think." Ephesians 3:20.

The New English Bible says He "is able to do *immeasurably more* than all we can ask or conceive."

Immeasurably more! That is exactly what He can do for us and wants to do for us. Why not make the most of His offer?

"Call unto Me," He said to the prophet Jeremiah while he was still in prison, "and I will answer thee, and show thee great and mighty things, which thou knowest not." Jeremiah 33:3.

What a wonderful invitation! All who accept it will see God work for them in marvelous ways.

In answer to Elijah's prayer fire fell from heaven.

"Lord God of Abraham, Isaac, and of Israel," he prayed, as he faced the fanatical priests of Baal on Carmel, "let it be known this day that Thou art God in Israel, and that I am Thy servant, and that I have done all these things at Thy word." 1 Kings 18:36.

It was a very simple prayer, but it revealed the complete consecration of the prophet, and his single-minded desire to bring honor to God's holy name. As a result, then and there, "the fire of the Lord fell."

King Hezekiah prayed a similar prayer when he received a letter from the king of Assyria demanding the immediate surrender of Jerusalem. He took the letter and "went up unto the house of the Lord, and spread it before the Lord. And Hezekiah prayed unto the Lord, saying, O Lord of hosts, God of Israel, that dwellest between the cherubims, Thou art the God, even Thou alone, of all the kingdoms of the earth: Thou hast made heaven and earth. Incline Thine ear, O Lord, and hear; open Thine eyes, O Lord, and see: and hear all the words of Sennacherib, which hath sent to reproach the living God. . . . Now therefore, O Lord our God, save us from his hand, that all the kingdoms of the earth may know that Thou art the Lord, even Thou only." Isaiah 37:14-20.

As a result of this prayer, which was also for the glory of God, the Assyrian army was mysteriously destroyed and Sennacherib returned to Nineveh without so much as shooting an arrow at Jerusalem.

Examples of great results from earnest prayers uttered by faith-filled men and women are not confined to Bible characters.

Many a servant of God in later years has witnessed similar divine intervention. The history of the church is replete with marvelous providences in answer to prayer. The life stories of missionaries like Livingstone and Moffat in Africa, of Morrison in China, and Judson in Burma are full of them.

Whenever men and women have pioneered for God in assisting the poor and needy, He has been especially near to them, laden with help and blessing.

Marvelous indeed is the story of George Müller and his orphanage, a philanthropic enterprise which has received over $9,000,000 solely in answer to prayer.

During World War II, when millions found themselves for the first time face to face with desperate danger, many turned to God for help and found Him a wonder-working Friend. Unforgettable are the stories of Lieutenant Whittaker and his companions who, on a life raft in the Pacific, prayed for water and saw a rain cloud come to them against the wind; of Major Allen Lindberg who in similar tragic plight prayed for deliverance and was providentially found by heathen tribesmen; of John Kennedy's rescue by Methodist and Seventh-day Adventist natives of the Solomon Islands.

Writing in the *American Magazine,* shortly after the war, Chaplain William C. Taggart said:

"I know of men lost and starving in the deserts of Australia who were found and brought to safety after asking God for help. Of men in bombers shot to pieces by enemy gunfire who, quite literally, prayed their way back to base. I know, too, that many times appeals uttered by mothers, wives, and sweethearts in the United States stretched a protective mantle half around the globe to shield us in the South Pacific.

"One high-ranking general told me that he owes his life, in part, to the petitions voiced by his closest friend and former business partner. I myself am living on borrowed time because my parents prayed for me in a situation of great danger."

I have been collecting answers to prayers for many

years. They come to me from fathers and mothers, boys and girls, all around the world. Scores of them I have retold in my books for children, such as *Bedtime Stories* and *The Children's Hour*. Together they present overwhelming evidence of God's constant love and watchcare over those who love and trust Him. They reveal that all around the globe there are still thousands upon thousands of sincere people who are daily seeking God in faith and finding Him not only a faithful Friend but "a very present help in trouble." Psalm 46:1.

He is ready to help you, too. Today, tomorrow, and through all the days to come.

Not every prayer will be answered, of course. And with good reason. Sometimes in our inexperience we ask for things which, if granted, would be positively harmful. Knowing this, He doesn't give them to us. Consequently we should always say, as Jesus did in Gethsemane, "Thy will be done." Matthew 26:42. Only as we ask "according to His will" does He hear us. 1 John 5:14.

Sometimes our prayers are purely selfish, and God doesn't answer that type, either. As James wrote: "You ask and do not receive, because you asked wrongly, to spend it on your passions." James 4:3, R.S.V.

Sometimes the fault lies deeper. "If I regard iniquity in my heart," said David, "the Lord will not hear me." Psalm 66:18. Unless we are truly sorry for our sins and genuinely want to be free from every evil thought we can hardly expect a pure and holy God to do much for us.

"Behold, the Lord's hand is not shortened, that it cannot save; neither His ear heavy, that it cannot hear," wrote Isaiah: "but your iniquities have separated between you and your God, and your sins have hid His face from you, that He will not hear." Isaiah 59:1, 2.

Much as God may wish to help us, cherished sin will keep Him from doing so. Like dirt in an electrical connection, sin stops the flow of power. Remove the dirt, give up the cherished sin, and the power will flow again.

We must be patient, too. Just because a prayer isn't answered immediately we must not assume that God will never answer it. "I waited patiently for the Lord," said David, "and He inclined unto me, and heard my cry." Psalm 40:1. We must trust God to answer at the right time and in a way that will be best for us.

So keep on praying. Whatever happens, keep up the good old habit of saying your prayers. "Pray without ceasing." 1 Thessalonians 5:17. This doesn't mean you must talk out loud to God all day long. It means living in a prayerful mood, thinking about God at every opportunity, being grateful to Him for all His goodness, quietly seeking His guidance and counsel about every problem. It means always, *habitually,* "casting all your care upon Him," knowing "He careth for you." 1 Peter 5:7.

Living, walking, communing with God like this will do more to ensure peace of mind in a time of trouble than anything else.

"Have no anxiety about anything," wrote the apostle Paul, "but in everything by prayer and . . . thanksgiving let your requests be made known to God. And the peace of God, which passes all understanding, will keep your hearts and your minds in Christ Jesus." Philippians 4:6, 7, R.S.V.

It will "keep" you from doubting, "keep" you from discouragement, "keep" you from despair.

As David wrote, "Wait on the Lord: be of good courage, and He shall strengthen thine heart." Psalm 27:14.

The law of Ten Commandments given to Moses on Mount Sinai is the most wonderful code of ethics in existence. God says He will write it in the hearts of all who love Him. Jeremiah 31:33.

BYRON DE BOLT

18

JOY FROM
OBEDIENCE

My STRENGTH is as the strength of ten, because my heart is pure," said Tennyson's Sir Galahad; and the principle here expressed is essential to buoyant, courageous living. No one can meet any issue adequately when burdened with a sense of guilt.

Nothing is more precious than a clear conscience. It puts a spring in the step and a gleam in the eye that wrongdoers can never know. Honesty, truthfulness, uprightness, send a man on his way with his shoulders back and his head held high, fearing nobody but God.

"Great peace have those who love Thy law," said the psalmist; "nothing can make them stumble." Psalm

119:165, R.S.V. Calmly they surmount every obstacle in their way. Nothing can stay their triumphant march toward the kingdom of God.

Doing what's right is a highly rewarding habit, ensuring happiness here and hereafter. Said the psalmist: "Blessed is the man who walks not in the counsel of the wicked, nor stands in the way of sinners, nor sits in the seat of scoffers; but his delight is in the law of the Lord, and on His law he meditates day and night. He is like a tree planted by streams of water, that yields its fruit in its season, and its leaf does not wither. In all that he does, he prospers." Psalm 1:1-3, R.S.V.

How can one be certain what is right and what is wrong?

The answer is a disciplined conscience. Not conscience by itself, for that would give a variety of answers, dependent upon one's background and upbringing. To be a trustworthy guide, conscience must be guided by "the law of the Lord." That is why study of this law is so vital. Only by constant meditation on it, "day and night," can the conscience react swiftly and decisively on the side of right.

To what law did the psalmist refer? Obviously the Ten Commandments, that great moral code given by God on Mount Sinai. He knew no other. To him this was the only faultless standard of righteousness. "The law of the Lord is perfect," he said, "converting the soul: the testimony of the Lord is sure, making wise the simple." Psalm 19:7.

Centuries later the apostle Paul described this same law as "holy, and just, and good" (Romans 7:12), while

James declared it to be "the perfect law of liberty." James 1:25.

Jesus had something to say about it, too. He told His disciples: "Do not suppose that I have come to abolish the law and the prophets; I did not come to abolish, but to complete. I tell you this: so long as heaven and earth endure, not a letter, not a stroke, will disappear from the law until all that must happen has happened." Matthew 5:17, 18, N.E.B.

With such strong New Testament backing it is no wonder that the Christian church adopted this code of ethics as its own. For centuries the beautiful Book of Common Prayer of the Church of England—and of Episcopalian churches around the world—has provided for the recital of the Ten Commandments at every Communion service, the congregation repeating after each commandment: "Lord, have mercy upon us, and incline our hearts to keep this law."

Most other churches, Protestant and Catholic, refer to this same moral law with like respect and reverence.

Charles Haddon Spurgeon, famous Baptist preacher, wrote: "There is not a commandment too many; there is not one too few; but it is so incomparable that its perfection is a proof of its divinity."—*Sermons*, vol. 2, p. 280.

Billy Graham has made similar glowing statements concerning the wonders of God's law. Thousands of other preachers have done the same and still take pride in paying tribute to this eternal, unchangeable standard of righteousness.

Let us look at these Ten Commandments again to

refresh our minds as to what God considers right and wrong. You will find them in Exodus 20:3-17. Here they are:

1. "Thou shalt have no other gods before Me."

This means that it is *right* to put God first in our lives and *wrong* to allow anyone else to take His place.

2. "Thou shalt not make unto thee any graven image, or any likeness of anything that is in heaven above, or that is in the earth beneath, or that is in the water under the earth: thou shalt not bow down thyself to them, nor serve them: for I the Lord thy God am a jealous God, visiting the iniquity of the fathers upon the children unto the third and fourth generation of them that hate Me; and showing mercy unto thousands of them that love Me, and keep My commandments."

This means that it is *right* to worship God as the Supreme Being, Lord of the universe, Creator of heaven and earth, and *wrong* to indulge in any form of idolatry. We must not bow down to idols, whether they be images, pictures, money, or any material possession.

3. "Thou shalt not take the name of the Lord thy God in vain; for the Lord will not hold him guiltless that taketh His name in vain."

This means that it is *right* to be reverent in all matters pertaining to God and *wrong* to be irreverent. We must not use His holy name as an idle swearword.

4. "Remember the Sabbath day, to keep it holy. Six days shalt thou labor, and do all thy work: but the seventh day is the Sabbath of the Lord thy God:

in it thou shalt not do any work, thou, nor thy son, nor thy daughter, thy manservant, nor thy maidservant, nor thy cattle, nor thy stranger that is within thy gates: for in six days the Lord made heaven and earth, the sea, and all that in them is, and rested the seventh day: wherefore the Lord blessed the Sabbath day, and hallowed it."

This means that it is *right* to observe the seventh day as the Sabbath of the Lord and *wrong* not to do so. It is *right* to engage in holy activities on this sacred day and *wrong* to use it for regular business purposes and the seeking of material gain.

5. "Honor thy father and thy mother: that thy days may be long upon the land which the Lord thy God giveth thee."

This means that it is *right* to honor our parents and *wrong* to treat them with disrespect. It is *right* to recognize their authority in the home, and *wrong* to disobey them. It is *right*—when they are old—to support them, and *wrong* to neglect them.

6. "Thou shalt not kill."

This means that it is *right* to value the lives of others as our own and *wrong* to have hatred and murder in our hearts.

7. "Thou shalt not commit adultery."

This means that it is *right* to be pure in every word and deed, and *wrong* to permit impure thoughts to enter our minds.

8. "Thou shalt not steal."

This means that it is *right* to be honest in all our business relationships and *wrong* to be dishonest.

9. "Thou shalt not bear false witness against thy neighbor."

This means that it is *right* to be truthful at all times and *wrong* to tell a lie.

10. "Thou shalt not covet thy neighbor's house, thou shalt not covet thy neighbor's wife, nor his manservant, nor his maidservant, nor his ox, nor his ass, nor anything that is thy neighbor's."

This means that it is *right* to be content with what God has given us, without envy toward those who are better off than ourselves, and *wrong* to be greedy and covetous.

Such is the standard of righteousness God gave to man thousands of years ago, a law so just and so all-embracing that it is now the basis of legal codes in all civilized nations. The more one meditates upon it the more wonderful it appears, for it gives evidence that its Author is aware of every weakness of the human heart.

Some people say, "We don't need this law nowadays, for Christ is our standard of righteousness. If we follow His example we shall never do wrong." Of course He is our example! But His perfect life did not nullify His law. It clarified it!

"He will magnify the law, and make it honorable," Isaiah predicted (Isaiah 42:21), and that is exactly what Jesus did. Who could have done it better? He was the Author of the law and understood more perfectly than anyone else the full purpose and intent of every clause.

Jesus kept the law flawlessly. Never once did He

break it in any respect. Said Peter: "He committed no sin, He was convicted of no falsehood." 1 Peter 2:22, N.E.B.

Looking at Jesus and the perfect life He lived should help us see more, not less, in the Ten Commandments. He showed how they were designed to be a marvelous law of love, calling for the utmost devotion to God and the good of one's fellow men. He revealed how He wants them to be kept, not by nominal compliance but by joyful obedience from love-filled hearts.

"O how love I Thy law!" exclaimed David. "It is my meditation all the day." Psalm 119:97. He had good reason for saying so. So have we. And the more we meditate upon it in the light of Christ's life and teachings the more we shall love it, too, and the more we shall want to observe its every precept with reverent care.

With this holy law in mind we shall never be in doubt or "in the dark," as to what is right and what is wrong. "The path of the just," the Bible says, "is as the shining light, that shineth more and more unto the perfect day." Proverbs 4:18. It is "like the light of dawn which shines brighter and brighter until full day." R.S.V.

Our greatest need is not for more knowledge concerning the law but for more strength to fulfill its requirements. Not for more light to see it, but for more power to keep it.

For no one can keep the law by himself. We may plan to keep it, resolve to keep it, and determine to keep it, only to fail miserably, just as the children of Israel did in the wilderness.

When Moses told them about the Ten Commandments they responded enthusiastically, "All that the Lord hath said will we do, and be obedient." Exodus 24:7.

That was the "old covenant," or agreement, and they broke it almost as soon as they had made it. They thought they could keep God's holy law in their own strength, and what a mess they made of things! That's why there had to be a new covenant, based on a better promise.

What was that?

"This shall be the covenant that I will make; . . . I will put My law in their inward parts, and *write it in their hearts;* and will be their God, and they shall be My people." Jeremiah 31:33.

Here is the secret of doing what is right habitually. God must write His law in our hearts. This done, conscience, guided and disciplined by that law, will keep us in the straight and narrow way. "Your ears shall hear a word behind you, saying, 'This is the way, walk in it,' when you turn to the right or when you turn to the left." Isaiah 30:21, R.S.V.

The same glorious truth was uttered by Jesus Himself when He said to His disciples: "If a man loves Me, he will keep My word, and My Father will love him, and We will come to him and make Our home with him." John 14:23, R.S.V.

When Father and Son, by the Holy Spirit, come into a person's heart, and make Their home there,

They bring not only the peace of heaven with Them, but its holiness and righteousness, too.

This miracle is a direct result of loving God and sincerely desiring to keep His word. He fills our hearts so completely with His love that we find ourselves doing right naturally, automatically, without thinking about it. Love, abounding and overflowing, becomes in very truth the "fulfilling of the law." Romans 13:10.

This doesn't mean that thereafter we shall never make a mistake. As long as we are human we shall never be infallible. But God has made provision for that. "If any man sin, we have an advocate with the Father, Jesus Christ the righteous." 1 John 2:1.

This assures us that if we do happen to stumble and fall we may get up and go on our way, rejoicing in the forgiving mercy of our Lord.

Thus by God's grace we may live a godly life. We may not only *know* what is right, but *do* it. We may have a clear conscience day by day. We may know the joy of obedience, of consciously living in harmony with God's will.

Thus, too, we may walk with God, as Enoch did in the long ago. And we may keep on walking with Him, in quiet confidence and courage, clear through the gathering storm into the calm of His kingdom beyond.

19

UPLIFT FROM WORSHIP

WHO has not felt a strange glow in the heart upon entering a building dedicated to the worship of God? Whether it be a spacious cathedral or a tiny wayside chapel, the quietness and peace of the place make one feel like saying with Jacob of old, "This is none other but the house of God, and this is the gate of heaven." Genesis 28:17.

Kneeling reverently in some such sanctuary turns the mind heavenward to contemplate the majesty and glory of the Eternal. Selfish thoughts fade. Contact with God is renewed.

Moments of true worship stand out in one's memory like glowing milestones along life's journey. I shall never forget the spiritual exhilaration experienced amid the majestic hush of Westminster Abbey, or listening to an anthem in New York's lovely Riverside Church, or just standing silently beside a lonely loch in the north of Scotland looking up beyond the stars.

At such sacred times the soul reaches out toward God, "lost in wonder, love, and praise," and is wondrously uplifted and blessed.

"The moments spent in worship are moments spent in contact with the great Reality of the universe and of life. What that may mean in liberation from sins and fears, in the release of hidden energies, in clarified mental and spiritual vision, in rested nerves, in the exaltation and integration of personality, in challenge to social action, in cultural development . . . is written in the secret annals of myriads of human lives."— S. A. Devan, *Ascent to Zion,* page 21.

Worship, to be truly effective, must be sincere. It must spring from a love-filled heart desirous of doing homage to the Lord of life.

Said Jesus to the woman of Samaria: "The time approaches, indeed it is already here, when those who are real worshipers will worship the Father in spirit and in truth. Such are the worshipers whom the Father wants. God is spirit, and those who worship Him must worship in spirit and in truth." John 4:23, 24, N.E.B.

The Jews of that day thought that worship must be in Jerusalem; the Samaritans insisted upon Samaria; but Jesus dismissed both claims as too petty for consideration. True worship, He said, could never be confined to "this mountain" or to Jerusalem (verse 21). God's children could worship Him anywhere.

It was the spirit, not the place, that mattered.

This was a new concept, glorious in its greatness. It has a message for us today. When the urge to worship comes upon us we may reach God instantly, wherever we happen to be. If we are near a church of our choice we may go in and "worship and bow down" and "kneel before the Lord our Maker" (Psalm 95:6); but if we are far from any man-made sanctuary we may do as Jacob did when he "worshiped, leaning upon the top of his staff." Hebrews 11:21.

Which suggests another comforting thought: Just as the place where one worships is of small concern to the Lord, so, too, is the position of the worshiper. One may "bow," or "kneel," or "lean;" all are acceptable to Him if the spirit is genuinely worshipful. Always it is the spirit that matters, not any outward form or ceremony.

Likewise no limitations have been set on the time of access to the holy of holies. All may come boldly to the throne of grace at any moment of the day or night, sure of the warmest welcome. Again it is the spirit, not the time of day, that is important.

This does not mean, of course, that there should be no specific times and places for worship. "The glorious liberty of the children of God" (Romans 8:21) should not be used as an excuse for failing to take advantage of all the special avenues of blessing He has provided.

The letter to the Hebrew Christians of the first century contains this good counsel: "Let us hold fast the confession of our hope without wavering, for He who promised is faithful; and let us consider how to

Going to church is another good habit that can
be a precious source of hope and courage. Worship brings one near to God, calming the mind
and refreshing the soul with spiritual strength.

F. P. G.

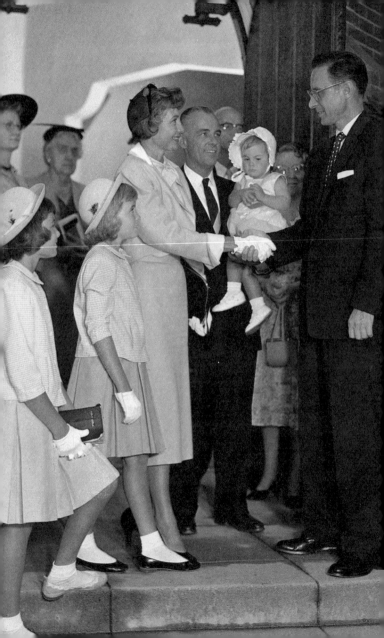

stir up one another to love and good works, *not neglecting to meet together,* as is the habit of some, but encouraging one another, and all the more as you see the day drawing near." Hebrews 10:23-25, R.S.V.

Even in those far-off days there were evidently some members who were "neglecting to meet together" or, as the New English Bible renders the phrase, "staying away from our meetings." By so doing they were both impoverishing their own hearts and robbing others of the encouragement their presence might have provided.

It is good to go to church. Good for you, and good for everybody else who sees you there. Individual worship at home, in the desert, or on the mountaintop, is a wonderful experience, but an extra blessing awaits those who gather in some dedicated sanctuary to "worship the Lord in the beauty of holiness." Psalm 96:9.

That God approves of regular collective worship is evident also from Malachi 3:16, 17: "They that feared the Lord spake often one to another: and the Lord hearkened, and heard it, and a book of remembrance was written before Him for them that feared the Lord, and that thought upon His name. And they shall be Mine, saith the Lord of hosts, in that day when I make up My jewels; and I will spare them, as a man spareth his own son that serveth him."

The size of the building does not matter, nor the number of people present. Even the smallest group may expect the presence of God. "For where two or three are gathered in My name," said Jesus, "there am I in the midst of them." Matthew 18:20, R.S.V.

It would seem from this precious promise that the very gathering together of Christians in the true spirit of worship invites the company of Jesus. He likes to be with those who love Him, and He brings with Him on every such occasion an abundance of encouragement and spiritual uplift.

So if your spirits are low and you cannot throw off your feelings of depression, try going to church. Failure to meet with others in worship may be the source of your trouble. Remember, too, that while one may worship God at any hour of the day or night and be richly rewarded for so doing; while one may, like Daniel, approach Him three times a day (Daniel 6:10) with one's windows open "toward Jerusalem;" God has made it very plain that there is one special time when a double blessing is available.

At the dawn of human history, after He had created this world and all its original forms of life, "He rested on the seventh day from all His work which He had made. And God blessed the seventh day, and sanctified it." Genesis 2:2, 3.

That was the beginning of that measurement of time we call "the week." It consisted of six working days followed by a rest day, or holy day.

The six working days belonged to man, but the seventh day belonged to God. As such it was to be devoted by man to fellowship with God, thinking about Him, talking to Him, praising Him, worshiping Him. It was "sanctified," or set apart for holy use. It was "blessed," or filled with blessing, by the very sacredness of its purpose. Man could not help but receive a double blessing as he spent this day in intimate communion with his Maker.

It was God's plan that the Sabbath should be completely different from all other days of the week. He was most specific on this point: "Remember the Sabbath day, to keep it holy," He said in the fourth commandment. "Six days shalt thou labor, and do all thy work: but the seventh day is the Sabbath of the Lord thy God: in it thou shalt not do any work, thou, nor thy son, nor thy daughter, thy manservant, nor thy maidservant, nor thy cattle, nor thy stranger that is within thy gates." Exodus 20:8-10.

He wanted nothing to disturb the peace and calm of this holy time. He wanted nothing to interrupt the precious, intimate contact between man and his God. He wanted nothing to hinder His people from receiving the fullness of blessing such as a day of worship would bring.

Worship on other days was not excluded, of course. Man could worship God each morning and evening if he so desired. He could have his personal worship and his family worship. But the seventh day was to be dedicated entirely to worship. From sunset on Friday evening until sunset on Saturday evening (for that is how it has been for many millenniums) no profane thoughts, no worldly activities, no seeking after material gain, was to keep him from contemplation of the goodness and glory of the Lord.

Long before there was a church, or a temple, or even a tabernacle, God said, "Six days shall work be done: but the seventh day is the Sabbath of rest, *an holy convocation;* ye shall do no work therein: it is the Sabbath of the Lord in all your dwellings." Leviticus 23:3.

Thus from those days of long ago the Sabbath has been "convocation day" or "meeting day"—the day when those who love God have gathered together to worship Him.

All down the centuries this beautiful custom has been followed. Jesus Himself observed it. At the very beginning of His earthly ministry "He came to Nazareth, where He had been brought up: and, as His custom was, He went into the synagogue on the Sabbath day, and stood up for to read." Luke 4:16.

He "went to synagogue on the Sabbath day as He regularly did," is the rendering of the New English Bible. This means He must have gone there over a thousand times between His boyhood days and the beginning of His ministry. With the mind's eye one can see Him walking there with His mother week after week, month after month, year after year, through childhood, youth, and manhood, going willingly, eagerly, happily, to worship His Father.

As the Author of the Sabbath He knew better than anyone else how it should be observed. Therefore by precept and example He showed men how they could worship not only by prayer and praise but also by revealing kindness and love to their fellow men. Purposely He performed some of His greatest miracles of healing on this day, to the mortification of the Pharisees and the joy of the common people. Gradually they perceived what a truly blessed and happy day the Sabbath was designed to be, a day dedicated exclusively to loving thoughts and kindly deeds. They saw that it was "sanctified" by love—love for God and love for man.

After spending more than three years with Jesus, His closest disciples considered the Sabbath so sacred a day that they would not even embalm His poor, mutilated body thereon. After Joseph of Arimathea had taken Him from the cross, the record says: "It was Friday, and the Sabbath was about to begin. The women who had accompanied Him from Galilee followed; they took note of the tomb and observed how His body was laid. Then they went home and prepared spices and perfumes; and on the Sabbath they rested in obedience to the commandment. But on the Sunday morning very early they came to the tomb bringing the spices they had prepared." Luke 23:54 to 24:1, N.E.B.

Even on that saddest of all Sabbaths, with the best possible excuse for working, the teaching and example of Jesus led them to rest and worship.

Leaders of the early church followed the same custom. When the apostle Paul arrived at Thessalonica he found a synagogue and, "as his manner was, went in unto them, and three Sabbath days reasoned with them out of the Scriptures." Acts 17:2.

"Following his usual practice Paul went to their meetings," says the New English Bible. The meaning is the same: Paul kept up the good old habit of going to church on the Sabbath day.

So did thousands of other Christians. And they

195

kept it up all down the centuries. It is a good habit to follow today. It calms the mind and refreshes the soul. It reopens the channels through which hope, strength, and courage flow into the human heart.

No wonder David wrote: "I was glad when they said unto me, Let us go into the house of the Lord." Psalm 122:1.

"How lovely is Thy dwelling place, O Lord of hosts!" the psalmist cried. "My soul longs, yea, faints for the courts of the Lord; my heart and flesh sing for joy to the living God. . . . For a day in Thy courts is better than a thousand elsewhere." Psalm 84:1-10, R.S.V.

"Extol the Lord our God," he exclaimed on another occasion. "Worship at His footstool! Holy is He!" Psalm 99:5, R.S.V.

Worship in this spirit, with fullness of love and devotion, will bring you near to God and God to you, as is so beautifully portrayed in the good old hymn by Edwin Barnes:

> O worship the Lord in the beauty of holiness,
>   Bow down before Him, His glory proclaim;
> With gold of obedience, and incense of lowliness,
>   Kneel and adore Him; the Lord is His name.
>
> Low at His feet lay thy burden of carefulness;
>   High on His heart He will bear it for thee,
> Comfort thy sorrows, and answer thy prayerfulness,
>   Guiding thy steps as may best for thee be.
>
> Fear not to enter His courts in the slenderness
>   Of the poor wealth thou wouldst reckon as thine.
> Truth in its beauty and love in its tenderness,
>   These are the offerings to lay on His shrine.

These, though we bring them in trembling and
fearfulness,
He will accept for the Name that is dear;
Mornings of joy give for evenings of tearfulness,
Trust for our trembling, and hope for our fear.

As the gathering storm approaches it would be well
to explore anew this oft-forgotten source of spiritual
strength and uplift. Worship "in spirit and in truth"
may well provide the help you need to carry you
through the coming crisis triumphantly.

20

VALOR FROM DEDICATION

CHRISTMAS, 1960, the
attention of millions was riveted upon a thrilling saga
of the sea. Two hundred miles off Cape Hatteras the
tanker "Pine Ridge" had broken in half in a storm.
The captain and six seamen had gone down with the
bow section. Surviving members of the crew had been
taken off by helicopters from the carrier "Valley Forge"
—all except Chief Engineer John Richard. As senior
officer left alive he felt he should try to bring what
remained of his shattered ship to port, or at least pro-
tect the owners' salvage rights.

It was one man against the sea, one man against the
fury of the elements, and he prevailed. Days later he

was still aboard when tugs towed the stricken vessel into drydock.

What made him do it? Dedication to duty.

About the same time John Brennan, fire chief of Bayonne, New Jersey, made his way through flames and exploding tanks to shut off a valve feeding a propane gas fire. With amazing gallantry he ignored the fearful peril to himself in order to prevent a major calamity to others.

Why? Dedication gave him valor.

Day by day during the disturbances in New Orleans the Reverend Lloyd A. Foreman took his little girl to school. With her hand in his he led her through the sneering, jeering mobs. Only a very brave man could have done that. Only someone deeply devoted to principle.

In New Hampshire recently, Dr. Willard Uplaus refused to reveal the names of persons who had attended a certain pacifist camp. Though sixty-nine and physically frail, he chose to go to prison rather than betray a confidence. "I stand upon my conscience," he told the legislature; "it is mean and contemptible to bring innocent people into public scorn and possible loss of livelihood."

Dedication inspired his gallantry. He went to jail, but history will take care of his reputation.

Not all heroes receive such publicity, yet the sacrificial deeds of the unknown are no less brave for lack of newspaper coverage.

Early in 1961 a father and mother escaped from their burning home only to discover that their children, through some misunderstanding, were still inside. Without a moment's hesitation they returned to the blazing bedroom and carried them out, just in time. Love made them fearless.

About the same time a seven-year-old boy, jumping on the faulty cover of a well, fell 250 feet down a twelve-inch casing. Instantly the father, who was standing nearby, offered to go down after him, head first, if necessary. Neighbors restrained him, while skillfully effecting a rescue with ropes. But the father's willingness to risk his life thrilled all who witnessed it. Devotion to his son made his own safety inconsequential.

When children are sick, mothers watch over them day after day and night after night without thought of their own weariness. In an epidemic doctors show similar selflessness in the care of their patients. In times of flood, fire, and earthquake, Red Cross and other social workers take all sorts of risks, and toil till they drop, to help homeless sufferers.

Whence springs this amazing valor? Chiefly from some loving purpose, some noble dedication.

People who go to pieces in a crisis are generally those who have been living self-centered, purposeless lives, dedicated to nothing in particular but their own selfish interests.

Intimately linked with faith, dedication enables a person to endure all manner of hardships without flinching. It spurs him to incredible feats of daring and sends him through fire and water with a smile on his face and a song in his heart.

The Bible abounds with records of men and women thus motivated.

"By faith Noah, divinely warned about the unseen future, took good heed and built an ark to save his household." Hebrews 11:7, N.E.B. Consider the stature of this man. He had never seen rain. Genesis 2:6. He did not know what the word "flood" meant. Yet in obedience to God's command he spent 120 years of his life building a great ship on dry land, to the vast amusement of his scoffing friends and neighbors. Only complete dedication could have given him the dogged persistence he needed to complete his task.

"By faith Abraham obeyed the call to go out to a land destined for himself and his heirs, and left home without knowing where he was to go. By faith he settled as an alien in the land promised him, living in tents, as did Isaac and Jacob, who were heirs to the same promise." Hebrews 11:8, 9, N.E.B.

Why did he go on this apparently futile journey? Why was he, a wealthy merchant of Ur of the Chaldees, willing to put up with all the inconveniences and uncertainties of a nomadic life? First, because he was sure God had spoken to him and he felt obligated to obey, and, second, because he detected a divine purpose to which he was willing to dedicate himself and his all. While he journeyed to Canaan, living in tents, "he was looking forward to the city with firm foundations, whose Architect and Builder is God." Verse 10, N.E.B.

"By faith Abraham, when the test came, offered up Isaac: he had received the promises, and yet he was on the point of offering his only son, of whom he had been told, 'Through the line of Isaac your posterity shall be traced.'" Verse 17, N.E.B.

So dearly did this good man love his son, so utterly dependent was he upon him for the future of his family name, that only total dedication to the will of God could have made him willing to make this supreme sacrifice. But even as he took the knife in his hand to slay the lad he reckoned by faith that God had power to bring him back from the dead if need be. Verse 19.

"By faith, when Moses was born, his parents hid him for three months, because they saw what a fine child he was; they were not afraid of the king's edict." Verse 23, N.E.B.

What courage that took, with Egyptian soldiers prowling everywhere in search of the newborn sons of the Hebrews! What dedication to the faith of their fathers and to the hope of the fulfillment of God's promises!

"By faith Moses, when he grew up, refused to be called the son of Pharaoh's daughter, preferring to suffer hardship with the people of God rather than enjoy the transient pleasures of sin." Verses 24, 25, N.E.B.

The words "refused" and "preferring" suggest a moment of great decision, the taking of a calculated risk. Deliberately Moses weighed all the pros and cons; on the one hand the fame and fortune awaiting him as Pharaoh's grandson, on the other the disgrace, torture, and death he knew all traitors received; and he decided for God. By some means he eluded the palace guards and fled the country. "Not because he feared the king's anger; for he was resolute, as one who saw the invisible God." Verse 27, N.E.B.

Trudging alone through the desert he was not discouraged. His soul soared above the mountains, for he had been true to his inner self, true to his destiny, true to his God. And the dedication that prompted his sacrifice led him to Sinai, Nebo, and heaven itself.

"By faith the walls of Jericho fell down after they had been encircled on seven successive days." Verse 30, N.E.B. Whose faith? In large measure Joshua's, of course—the man who accepted the scepter of leadership from Moses and led Israel across Jordan into the Promised Land. "Only be thou strong and very courageous," he had been bidden, and that he tried to be. Fearlessly, with one consuming purpose, he went from victory to victory till all the land was conquered.

As century succeeded century innumerable heroes appeared, performing great feats of daring. The Bible says, "Time is too short . . . to tell the stories of Gideon, Barak, Samson, and Jephthah, of David and Samuel and the prophets. Through faith they overthrew kingdoms, established justice, saw God's promises fulfilled. They muzzled ravening lions, quenched the fury of fire, escaped death by the sword. Their weakness was turned to strength, they grew powerful in war, they put foreign armies to rout." Verses 32-35, N.E.B. In every case the secret of valor was dedication to a great purpose, coupled with faith in the power and love of God.

Noblest example of all, of course, was Jesus Christ Himself, who "for the sake of the joy that lay ahead of Him, endured the cross, making light of its disgrace." Hebrews 12:2, N.E.B. Though one with God, with supreme self-abnegation He "made Himself nothing. . . . He humbled Himself, and in obedience accepted even death—death on a cross." Philippians 2:7, 8, N.E.B.

He "did not come to be served but to serve, and to surrender His life as a ransom for many." Mark 10:45, N.E.B.

Total dedication nerved Him to endure the utmost in suffering while giving the utmost in selfless service.

Disciples by thousands followed in His footsteps, both to the cross and to the grave. Gladly they endured all manner of torments for His name's sake. Like the apostle Paul, they reckoned "everything sheer loss" for the joy of knowing and serving Him. Philippians 3:8, N.E.B.

As the early centuries of the Christian Era merged into the Dark Ages the "noble army of martyrs" grew by leaps and bounds. As noted in a previous chapter, multitudes of godly men, women, and children suffered unspeakable cruelties rather than deny their faith in the simple truths of Christ's kingdom of love. "They were stoned, they were sawn in two, they were put to the sword." They were stretched on the rack. They were buried alive. They were burned at the stake. But they refused to deny their Lord. Faith kept them loyal. Dedication gave them valor.

We need such courage today. Indeed, "the times,

poised on the edge of space, imbued with brighter promise and blackened with direr threat than any we have known, are propitious for it."—*Life* magazine, January 6, 1961.

Says President Kennedy in *Profiles in Courage:* "Only the very courageous will be able to take the hard and unpopular decisions necessary for our survival in the struggle with a powerful enemy."— Page 19.

The real contest behind the struggle he mentions is described in Bible prophecy in the following dramatic language: "The dragon grew furious with the woman, and went off to wage war on the rest of her offspring, that is, on those who keep God's commandments and maintain their testimony to Jesus." Revelation 12:17, N.E.B.

The dragon is the devil, or Satan, the prince of darkness, and the instigator and fomenter of all the strife and evil in the world. The woman is the true church, and "the rest of her offspring" are those who "keep God's commandments and maintain their testimony to Jesus" in the last days of the world's history.

The struggle between the two is not new. It has been going on since the dawn of time. It has been the basic conflict of the ages. The only difference now is that its climax is approaching. Hence the gathering storm. Hence "the crisis at the close" in which we find ourselves and which daily increases in complexity and severity.

Darker than many have supposed are the days immediately ahead. As the fury of the dragon mounts against the remnant of the true church, some inevitably will suffer great hardship and loss. But faith will give courage to endure the worst. Dedication will inspire valor for glorious exploits for God.

"Here the fortitude of God's people has its place—in keeping God's commands and remaining loyal to Jesus." Revelation 14:12, N.E.B.

Fortitude! That is what we need. And that is what we may have.

If we give ourselves to Jesus in full and glad surrender, if we resolve by His grace to do what is right and follow in His steps, if we daily, *habitually*, rededicate ourselves to Him and His service, our strength will be ample for all our needs. Trusting in His promises, sure of His victory, we may face the future without a fear.

Part Five

∿∿∿∿∿∿∿∿∿∿∿∿∿∿∿∿∿∿

COURAGE FROM GREAT CERTAINTIES

As Daniel interpreted Nebuchadnezzar's dream, the two men beheld a panorama of all history to be. Beyond Babylon, Medo-Persia, Greece, and Rome they saw modern Europe and the kingdom of God.

KEN GUNALL, ARTIST   © P. P. P. A.

21

GOD'S VICTORY SURE

*I*N TIMES of turmoil and confusion it is wondrously comforting to rest one's faith upon some great certainty, to trust with implicit confidence in a promise that cannot fail.

I well recall how, early in World War II, when Hitler was on the rampage in Europe, his swift conquests striking fear into the hearts of millions, I wrote an editorial for the *Signs of the Times* declaring categorically that this would-be conqueror of the continent would fail in his objective.

At that moment the suggestion was so contrary to the obvious trend of events that friends urged me not to print it. Some even tried to persuade the publishers to keep it out of the journal. The risk of contradiction was too great, they said. But the article appeared and many a worried reader was consoled thereby. Four years later Hitler was dead amid the ruins of the empire he had sought in vain to build.

My conviction was based not upon any findings of political science, or the lessons of history, but rather upon a clear statement of Holy Scripture, a revelation so definite and unequivocal that—as we shall see later— it allows for no doubt whatever.

It is one of the great certainties of the Bible, set forth dramatically, in story form, in the second chapter of the book of Daniel. We need to study it anew today when evil forces are once more on the march, with world domination their acknowledged goal.

It has a mighty message of courage for every fearful heart, declaring that all despots and dictators are destined to total eclipse. Their transient empires shall be ground to dust and the final victory shall be not theirs but God's.

This remarkable story has been retold times without number down the centuries but never loses its forcefulness. It concerns two young men. One was Nebuchadnezzar, king of Babylon, and the other was Daniel, a prince of Israel, who had recently been taken prisoner during an assault on Jerusalem.

One youth was ruler of the greatest empire of ancient times, the other a captive slave. That they should meet at all was a strange coincidence; but that they should confront each other in the royal palace under the circumstances described in such lavish detail in this story was an amazing miracle of divine providence.

It happened like this: One night the young king had a dream which made a great impression on his mind. By morning he had forgotten it. All that remained was a conviction that it had some profound significance.

The more he tried to recall the dream the more frustrated he became. At last he decided to seek help from his counselors, including "the magicians, and the astrologers, and the sorcerers," and other dealers in the occult.

"Tell us the dream," they said, "and we will interpret it."

"That's the trouble," said the king, in effect. "I can't. The thing is gone from me."

Now the counselors were in real trouble. They could concoct an interpretation without difficulty, but to describe the dream itself was something else again. It was too easy to guess wrong.

"Nobody can do this," they said, "nor has any king asked such a thing of any magician or astrologer before."

The king coaxed. He offered bribes. But to no effect. The counselors were helpless.

Losing patience, he began to threaten. If they did not tell him his dream he would have them cut in pieces and their houses destroyed. Still they were silent.

At last, becoming "very furious," he called the captain of the guard and gave orders that all the wise men of Babylon should be slain.

At this point Daniel entered the picture. Because

211

of his proven sagacity his name had already been added to the list of the city's wise men. Consequently the guard turned up at his door to arrest him.

Shocked by the drastic nature of the order, Daniel pleaded for time, promising the king that he would be told his dream.

Now he had to deliver, and fast. Calling three of his Hebrew friends together, he sought God earnestly for help. That night he was shown both the king's dream and its interpretation.

"Blessed be the name of God forever and ever," he cried out in heartfelt gratitude: "for wisdom and might are His: and He changeth the times and the seasons: He removeth kings, and setteth up kings: He giveth wisdom unto the wise, and knowledge to them that know understanding: He revealeth the deep and secret things: He knoweth what is in the darkness, and the light dwelleth with Him. I thank Thee, and praise Thee, O Thou God of my fathers, who hast given me wisdom and might, and hast made known unto me now what we desired of Thee: for Thou hast now made known unto us the king's matter." Daniel 2:20-23.

Ushered into the presence of Nebuchadnezzar, the young captive stood before him without fear. Having talked with the King of kings, why should he quail before the ruler of an earthly empire? Nor did he question for one moment that the dream he was about to recite was correct in every detail.

"Can you tell me my dream?" asked Nebuchadnez-zar.

"I can't," said Daniel humbly, "but God can. There

is a God in heaven who reveals secrets, and makes known to King Nebuchadnezzar what shall be in the latter days."

He then recounted the dream.

"Thou, O king, sawest, and behold a great image," he said, as the king leaned forward with ever-increasing fascination. "This great image, whose brightness was excellent, stood before thee; and the form thereof was terrible.

"This image's head was of fine gold, his breast and his arms of silver, his belly and his thighs of brass, his legs of iron, his feet part of iron and part of clay.

"Thou sawest till that a stone was cut out without hands, which smote the image upon his feet that were of iron and clay, and brake them to pieces.

"Then was the iron, the clay, the brass, the silver, and the gold, broken to pieces together, and became like the chaff of the summer threshing floors; and the wind carried them away, that no place was found for them: and the stone that smote the image became a great mountain, and filled the whole earth." Verses 31-35.

The light in the king's eyes and the glow upon his face must have been something to see. For this was exactly what he had beheld in his dream, in all its gripping reality.

Silent in wonder, he waited for this extraordinary youth to proceed.

"This is the dream," continued Daniel; "and we will tell the interpretation thereof before the king." Verse 36.

Humbly, sincerely, confidently, he proceeded to impart the most startling revelation ever made to a heathen monarch:

"Thou, O king, art a king of kings: for the God of heaven hath given thee a kingdom, power, and strength, and glory. And wheresoever the children of men dwell, the beasts of the field and the fowls of the heaven hath He given into thine hand, and hath made thee ruler over them all. Thou art this head of gold.

"And after thee shall arise another kingdom inferior to thee, and another third kingdom of brass, which shall bear rule over all the earth.

"And the fourth kingdom shall be strong as iron: forasmuch as iron breaketh in pieces and subdueth all things: and as iron that breaketh all these, shall it break in pieces and bruise.

"And whereas thou sawest the feet and toes, part of potters' clay, and part of iron, the kingdom shall be divided; but there shall be in it of the strength of the iron, forasmuch as thou sawest the iron mixed with miry clay.

"And as the toes of the feet were part of iron, and part of clay, so the kingdoms shall be partly strong, and partly broken.

"And whereas thou sawest iron mixed with miry clay, they shall mingle themselves with the seed of men: but they shall not cleave one to another, even as iron is not mixed with clay.

"And in the days of these kings shall the God of heaven set up a kingdom, which shall never be destroyed: and the kingdom shall not be left to other people, but it shall break in pieces and consume all these kingdoms, and it shall stand forever.

"Forasmuch as thou sawest that the stone was cut out of the mountain without hands, and that it brake in pieces the iron, the brass, the clay, the silver, and the gold; the great God hath made known to the king what shall come to pass hereafter: and *the dream is certain, and the interpretation thereof sure.*" Verses 37-45.

Suddenly these two young men found themselves gazing upon a panorama never before seen by human eyes. For this was no mere recital of a dream; it was a revelation of all history to be.

As the veil of the future was mysteriously withdrawn, they looked out together across the vast expanse of unborn centuries. They saw the rise and fall of kingdoms yet to be. They saw unknown conquerors come and go. They beheld the strife and turmoil of rival nations in our time. And they gazed at last upon the King of kings coming in power and glory to set up a kingdom which shall endure forever.

Sublime, magnificent vista!

No wonder Nebuchadnezzar exclaimed in mingled amazement and humility: "Of a truth it is, that your God is a God of gods, and a Lord of kings, and a revealer of secrets." Verse 47.

That was in 603 B.C. Twenty-five centuries have passed since then—centuries that could so easily have proved Daniel's interpretation both false and foolish. They did not. Instead, every detail has come to pass; everything, that is, except God's final victory.

Four world empires have come upon the stage of history, exactly as predicted.

When Babylon's day was done the scepter passed to Medo-Persia, inferior in wealth and majesty as silver is to gold, but greater far in strength. Then followed Greece, the mighty kingdom of brass, led by Alexander the Great.

Disintegrating in time, Greece gave place to Rome, the fourth kingdom which, strong as iron, broke in pieces and completely subdued the whole Mediterranean world.

In course of time Rome, too, came to its end. Weakened by internal corruption, hard-pressed by barbarian tribes, it fell apart into ten divisions, namely, the Anglo-Saxons, the Franks, the Alamanni, the Lombards, the Ostrogoths, the Visigoths, the Burgundians, the Vandals, the Suevi, and the Heruli. Seven of these may be clearly traced to the nations of modern Europe.

For nigh fifteen hundred years these fragments of iron and clay have been in existence, with one strong man after another striving in vain to unite them again into one great whole. Time and again the attempt has been made—by Charlemagne, by Charles V, by Louis XIV, by Napoleon, by Kaiser Wilhelm—but every one has failed. Some tried treaties, some tried intermarriage, some tried war, but all came to the same frustrating end. Blocking every attempt at reunion were the seven fateful words of the divine edict: *"They shall not cleave one to another."*

These are the words that defeated Hitler and all the great conquerors who preceded him. They are the words which will bring to ruin every aspirant to European or world dominion who may arise in the future.

True, some unusually fearsome character may temporarily impose his will on other nations, but sooner or later his grandiose plans will come crashing down in total disaster.

When perplexed as to the outcome of international conflicts, rival ideologies, and bitter racial disputes, read these words again, and the striking prediction which follows them: "In the days of these kings [kingdoms] shall the God of heaven set up a kingdom, which shall never be destroyed."

This will be the ultimate outcome.

While Rome remains divided, God will intervene in the affairs of men to bring all earthly kingdoms to an end. The Stone "cut out without hands" will smite the image *"upon his feet"* and break them in pieces, then fill "the whole earth" with the glory of the Lord. Verses 34, 35.

Glorious certainty! How it should cheer our hearts in the darkest and most evil times!

God's victory is sure!

As certainly as Medo-Persia followed Babylon in the sequence of empires; as certainly as Greece took Medo-Persia's place; as certainly as Rome seized the scepter from Greece; as certainly as Rome remains divided to this day; so certainly the final event of human history will be Christ's coming in glory to establish His eternal kingdom of righteousness and peace.

There can be no possible doubt about it. "The dream is certain, and the interpretation thereof sure."

22

RIGHT SHALL PREVAIL

*I*N 1845, a year of many political revolutions, James Russell Lowell wrote his famous poem on freedom, containing the immortal lines:

> Truth forever on the scaffold, Wrong forever on the throne,—
> Yet that scaffold sways the future, and, behind the dim unknown,
> Standeth God within the shadow, keeping watch above His own.

Today, over a century later, these words are as true as when Lowell wrote them; and they are likely to become more so as the gathering storm bursts upon us in all its fury.

Well may we see truth on the scaffold and wrong on the throne to an extent never before known in history.

The prospect would be discouraging indeed but for the divine assurance that this state of affairs will not continue forever. Someday it will be completely reversed. Wrong shall be condemned and truth exalted. As certain as tomorrow's dawn, right shall ultimately prevail.

This truth is emphasized over and over again in the Holy Scriptures, but nowhere more clearly than in the seventh chapter of the book of Daniel.

Here again is portrayed the course of history from the days of Babylon to the end of time, with additional facts of great importance.

In this second revelation of the future the great empires of prophecy passed before Daniel not as parts of a metallic image but as four ferocious beasts which emerged from the wild waves of a stormy sea.

As he stood upon a windswept shore he saw a strange creature padding up out of the water. It resembled a lion, but had two wings like an eagle. In a little while the queer creature raised itself up on its hind legs and its wings fell off.

Behind it came a bear with three ribs in its mouth. It was humped up on one side as though two legs were longer than the others.

Next came a leopard, with four heads and four wings, and finally a fourth beast so "dreadful and terrible" that Daniel couldn't think of a name for it. It had ten horns and great iron teeth.

Soon something strange began to happen on the beast's head. A little horn rose among the ten, pushing out three of them and developing "eyes like the eyes of a man, and a mouth speaking great things."

Suddenly the prophet's attention was called from this extraordinary sequence of events to a scene infinitely more fascinating. Looking upward, he found himself gazing into heaven. On a glorious throne ringed with "fiery flame" sat "the Ancient of Days" while "thousand thousands ministered unto Him, and ten thousand times ten thousand stood before Him: the judgment was set, and the books were opened." Daniel 7:10.

The case before the court was that of the fourth beast and the wicked words uttered by the horn upon its head. The verdict was "guilty" and the sentence was "death." Daniel watched until "the beast was slain, and his body destroyed, and given to the burning flame" that flashed forth from the throne of God.

The rest of the beasts were also punished, and all the power and glory they had ever had was bestowed upon "one like the Son of man," who "came with the clouds of heaven, . . . to the Ancient of Days. . . . And there was given Him dominion, and glory, and a kingdom, that all people, nations, and languages, should serve Him: His dominion is an everlasting dominion, which shall not pass away, and His kingdom that which shall not be destroyed." Verses 13, 14.

Quite naturally Daniel was troubled, wondering what it all meant. He prayed for understanding that he might know "the truth of all this." Help soon came.

A heavenly being summed up the vision in two brief verses: "These great beasts, which are four, are four kings, which shall arise out of the earth. But the saints of the Most High shall take the kingdom, and possess the kingdom forever, even forever and ever." Verses 17, 18.

Daniel wasn't satisfied. He wanted to know more about that fourth beast which was so different from the others and behaved with such ferocity. The great horn worried him, too, with its cruel stare and blasphemous words.

The angel answered: "The fourth beast shall be the fourth kingdom upon earth, which shall be diverse from all kingdoms, and shall devour the whole earth, and shall tread it down, and break it in pieces.

"And the ten horns out of this kingdom are ten kings that shall arise: and another shall rise after them; and he shall be diverse from the first, and he shall subdue three kings.

"And he shall speak great words against the Most High, and shall wear out the saints of the Most High, and think to change times and laws: and they shall be given into his hand until a time and times and the dividing of time.

"But the judgment shall sit, and they shall take away his dominion, to consume and to destroy it unto the end." Verses 23-26.

As we look back across the centuries there is no problem in identifying the symbols employed in this prophecy.

Obviously the four beasts represent the same four

empires pictured in the image of Nebuchadnezzar's dream, namely, Babylon, Medo-Persia, Greece, and Rome.

The head of gold, which symbolized Babylon, is here referred to as a lion with eagle's wings.

The breast and arms of silver, which represented Medo-Persia, are now a bear with three ribs in its mouth.

The belly and thighs of brass, which stood for Greece, correspond to the leopard with four heads and four wings.

The legs of iron, which would "break in pieces" and bruise all opponents—so fitting a symbol of Rome—are identical with the fourth beast "dreadful and terrible, and strong exceedingly" which "devoured and brake in pieces, and stamped the residue with the feet of it."

The feet and toes of the image find their counterpart in the ten horns on the fourth beast and the ten divisions of the Roman Empire.

Here the similarities end and a new power is introduced.

Depicted as a little horn growing up among the ten, it came on the stage of history at approximately the same time as they did. Quickly it dominated the scene, occupying the seat of the Caesars and exercising powers no emperor ever claimed. It was "diverse" from the others in that, while resembling a political organization, it assumed religious aspects, the resultant combination of church and state bringing upon the true saints of God the worst persecution known to man and stamping the era of its supremacy as the Dark Ages of history.

Closer identification of this power is not necessary here. Readers who would pursue this phase of the subject further may do so in the author's *God and the Future*. What concerns us at this moment is the great truth behind this remarkable prediction: All despotisms, whether political or religious, or a combination of both, must someday face the judgment seat of God.

Sometimes it may seem as though God takes no notice of their blasphemies and cruelties. But He does. Every wicked word is recorded. So is every ugly deed. And when the books of heaven are opened there will be a heavy price to pay.

Wrong may be on the throne today, but it will be in the fire tomorrow, "given to the burning flame."

Truth may be on the scaffold today, but it will be victorious at last.

Concerning the "little horn" itself, symbol of the worst tyranny that ever dominated the lives and fortunes of men, the prophecy says: "The judgment shall sit, and they shall take away his dominion, to consume and to destroy it unto the end." Verse 26.

Such will be the fate of this monstrous religio-political despotism, and of all tyrannies, present and future. The judgment will decide against them. They shall be consumed and destroyed until there is nothing left of them, not even a memory.

And after that? "The kingdom and dominion, and the greatness of the kingdom under the whole heaven, shall be given to the people of the saints of the Most High, whose kingdom is an everlasting kingdom, and all dominions shall serve and obey Him." Verse 27.

Surely God could not have outlined more definitely the outcome of the agelong controversy between right and wrong. Nor could He have described more clearly the totality of the triumph that awaits all who love and serve Him. Nothing less than the "greatness of the kingdom under the whole heaven" shall be theirs forevermore.

Right shall prevail. Gloriously. Universally.

Never doubt it.

Like a peal of victory bells the thrilling assurance comes ringing down the centuries to cheer our hearts today.

Hear it from the great apostle to the Gentiles: "Then cometh the end, when He shall have delivered up the kingdom to God, even the Father; when He shall have put down all rule and all authority and power. For He must reign." 1 Corinthians 15:24, 25.

Hear it from the angels in glory: "I heard the voice of many angels round about the throne: . . . And every creature which is in heaven, and on the earth, and under the earth, and such as are in the sea, and all that are in them, heard I saying, Blessing, and honor, and glory, and power, be unto Him that sitteth upon the throne, and unto the Lamb forever and ever." Revelation 5:11-13.

What a thrilling certainty is this! With such infallible promises to sustain us we need never flinch or quail before the worst threatenings of wicked men, or the greatest aggregations of evil power. Beyond the strife, the storm, and the crisis lies a victory we may share.

23

EVIL SHALL PERISH

NOT only are despotisms of every kind doomed to extinction, all wickedness will one day follow them into oblivion.

Evil shall perish.

This is the clear teaching of Holy Scripture and another of the great certainties which should sustain our courage in the dark days ahead.

True, at the moment, the wicked are "in great power" and spread themselves "like a green bay tree." Psalm 37:35. True, this sad state of affairs will get worse before it gets better. As the apostle Paul wrote: "Evil men and seducers shall wax worse and worse, deceiving, and being deceived." 2 Timothy 3:13. But this will not continue forever. Were it to do so, the outlook would be utterly discouraging. Life would not be worth living. Justice, honesty, truth, and virtue, already in jeopardy, would completely disappear. The devil would triumph and all hell break loose.

The gathering storm may bring us to the brink of such disaster, but no further, for God has decreed otherwise.

Someday soon the tide of lawlessness will be turned back. Suddenly, violently, the power of evil will be broken, once and for all.

Consider these inspired assurances, first, from the psalms of David:

"The face of the Lord is against them that do evil, to cut off the remembrance of them from the earth." Psalm 34:16.

"For evildoers shall be cut off. . . . For yet a little while, and the wicked shall not be: yea, thou shalt diligently consider his place, and it shall not be." Psalm 37:9, 10.

"But Thou, O God, shalt bring them down into the pit of destruction." Psalm 55:23.

Solomon was equally definite: "The wicked shall be cut off from the earth," he wrote, "and the transgressors shall be rooted out of it." Proverbs 2:22.

In picturesque but most explicit language the prophet Hosea said that the wicked "shall be as the *morning cloud,* and as the *early dew* that passeth away, as *the chaff* that is driven with the whirlwind out of the floor, and as the *smoke out of the chimney.*" Hosea 13:3.

Equally definite was the prophet Malachi. He said: "For, behold, the day cometh, that shall burn as an oven; and all the proud, yea, and all that do wickedly, shall be stubble: and the day that cometh shall *burn them up,* saith the Lord of hosts, that it shall leave them neither root nor branch." Malachi 4:1.

Admittedly these are all Old Testament quotations. What about the New? There is no difference.

When John the Baptist alerted his listeners about the coming of the Messiah he said: "I indeed baptize you with water unto repentance: but He that cometh after me is mightier than I: . . . whose fan is in His hand, and He will throughly purge His floor, and gather His wheat into the garner; but He will *burn up the chaff with unquenchable fire.*" Matthew 3: 11, 12.

Did Jesus teach this, too? He surely did.

Explaining His parable of the wheat and tares to His disciples, He made crystal clear what the fate of the obstinately wicked will be:

"He that soweth the good seed is the Son of man," He said; "the field is the world; the good seed are the children of the kingdom; but the tares are the children of the wicked one; the enemy that sowed them is the devil; the harvest is the end of the world; and the reapers are the angels. As therefore the tares are gathered and burned in the fire; so shall it be in the end of this world. The Son of man shall send forth His angels, and they shall gather out of His kingdom all things that offend, and them which do iniquity; and shall cast them *into a furnace of fire.*" Matthew 13:37-42.

In harmony with this the apostle Peter declared that "the heavens and the earth, which are now, by the same word are kept in store, reserved unto fire against the day of judgment and perdition of ungodly men." 2 Peter 3:7.

If there is delay in bringing about the end of evil, he added, it will not be a result of God's indifference, but because of His long-suffering love. "The Lord is not slack concerning His promise, as some men count slackness," he said; "but is long-suffering to usward, not willing that any should perish, but that all should come to repentance." Verse 9.

Eventually, however, God's purpose will be accomplished. The devil and all his works will be brought to nought. "The day of the Lord will come as a thief in the night; in the which the heavens shall pass away with a great noise, and the elements shall melt with fervent heat, the earth also and the works that are therein shall be burned up." Verse 10.

In the book of Revelation the apostle John gives the final touch of certainty to all this in the nineteenth and twentieth chapters.

First, he tells how "the beast" and the "false prophet " will be "cast alive into a lake of fire." Revelation 19:20. Then he pictures the ultimate fate of Satan and all the hosts of evil.

Led by the prince of darkness, these wicked multitudes will compass "the camp of the saints about, and the beloved city," whereupon fire will come down "from God out of heaven" and devour them. Revelation 20:9.

The Bible is absolutely positive that evil will come to an end. Not by the conversion of Satan and his followers, but by their total elimination from the universe. God will remove their blighting influence once for all.

This was one of the chief reasons why Jesus came from heaven to earth: "For this purpose the Son of God was manifested, that He might destroy the works of the devil." 1 John 3:8.

And a thorough job will He make of it. Not only will He destroy the *works* of the devil, but the devil himself. "And the devil that deceived them" will be cast into "the lake of fire." Revelation 20:10.

As a result, the day will dawn when "there shall be no more curse" (Revelation 22:3), and no more "utter destruction" (Zechariah 14:11); and "the former" things—all the mean, ugly, hateful things— "shall not be remembered, nor come into mind." Isaiah 65:17.

Perhaps you have been puzzled by the term "everlasting fire," which occurs in Matthew 18:8 and 25:41, and assumed from these passages that evil will continue forever, albeit in perpetual disgrace and torment. This is an incorrect deduction. It is the *effect* of the fire, not the fire itself, that lasts forever.

Thus Sodom and Gomorrah suffered "the vengeance of eternal fire" (Jude 7), though the Dead Sea now covers the site where these cities once stood.

Likewise, when Jesus said that the wicked will be cast into "hell" (Greek, Gehenna) "where their worm dieth not, and the fire is not quenched" (Mark 9:48), He used the familiar illustration of a city dump to describe the ultimate fate of those who reject God's mercy. Both fire and worms will continue their cleansing task until it is completed.

All connected with the great rebellion against the good government of God, whether in the beginning or now, whether angels or men, will ultimately vanish as "smoke out of the chimney." They will be so completely consumed that there shall be left "neither root nor branch." Only those who accept the gracious offer of salvation through Jesus Christ will escape.

In the light of these facts new meaning glows in the glorious words: "God so loved the world, that He gave His only-begotten Son, that whosoever believeth in Him *should not perish,* but have everlasting life." John 3:16.

God is love. He does not want anyone to perish. He yearns to give life, not death. "Have I any pleasure in the death of the wicked, says the Lord God, and not rather that he should turn from his way and live?" Ezekiel 18:23, R.S.V. So He offers this way of escape. It is still open. He continues to wait in long-suffering compassion for men and women to turn to Him. But He will not wait forever. He cannot and will not permit evil to continue throughout eternity. Someday He will cleanse His universe from every trace of it.

Glorious certainty! How it should fortify us for the trials and struggles ahead! Let the wicked seize the seats of power. Let them spread themselves like a green bay tree. Let them scoff at truth and mock at goodness. It will not be for long. Their days are numbered. Their end is near.

Despite all the fearful happenings of earth's final crisis thousands of faithful Christians will survive to welcome their returning Lord, saying, "This is our God; we have waited for Him, and He will save us."

24

CHRIST WILL RETURN

*F*ROM the earliest times good men and women have looked forward eagerly to the coming of Christ in glory to this earth.

To all it was a sure and certain hope which brought great peace and comfort to their hearts. They did not know when it would happen, but they never doubted that it would mark the climax of history and the triumph of good over evil.

The Bible says that Enoch, "the seventh from Adam" left on record this prediction: "Behold, the Lord cometh with ten thousands of His saints, to execute judgment upon all, and to convince all that are ungodly among them of all their ungodly deeds which they have ungodly committed, and of all their hard speeches which ungodly sinners have spoken against Him." Jude 14, 15.

"I saw the Lord come with His myriads of angels, to bring all men to judgment," is the rendering of the New English Bible, and it is thrilling indeed to think that this man of God had such a vision well over five thousand years ago.

In the book of Job, believed to be the oldest of all the books of the Bible, we find the hard-pressed patriarch saying: "I know that my Redeemer liveth, and that He shall stand at the latter day upon the earth: and though after my skin worms destroy this body, yet in my flesh shall I see God: whom I shall see for myself, and mine eyes shall behold, and not another." Job 19:25-27.

This was the blessed hope which buoyed up his spirits, enabling him to carry his incredibly heavy burdens and to say with resolute devotion, "Though He slay me, yet will I trust in Him." Job 13:15.

In later years the prophets of Israel were led to explain that there would be two divine visits to this earth, the first in humility and suffering, the second in power and glory.

Isaiah foretold the coming of One who would be "despised and rejected of men; a Man of Sorrows, and acquainted with grief," who would be "wounded for our transgressions," and "bruised for our iniquities." But he also looked far beyond this time of sacrifice and sorrow to a day of triumph and rejoicing.

The day will dawn, he said, when the Lord will

"destroy in this mountain the face of the covering cast over all people, and the veil that is spread over all nations. He will swallow up death in victory; and the Lord God will wipe away tears from off all faces; and the rebuke of His people shall He take away from off all the earth." Isaiah 25:7, 8.

As we have seen in previous chapters, the prophet Daniel bore similar witness, declaring that all earthly empires shall one day give place to the kingdom of God, with all dominion "under the whole heaven" being given to "the people of the saints of the Most High." Daniel 7:27.

This cheering message, in many forms, appears over and over in the Old Testament and is found many times in the New.

It is one of the main themes of Paul's epistles. To the Thessalonians he gave this assurance: "For the Lord Himself shall descend from heaven with a shout, with the voice of the Archangel, and with the trump of God: and the dead in Christ shall rise first: then we which are alive and remain shall be caught up together with them in the clouds, to meet the Lord in the air: and so shall we ever be with the Lord." 1 Thessalonians 4:16, 17.

To Titus he wrote: "For the grace of God that bringeth salvation hath appeared to all men, teaching us that, denying ungodliness and worldly lusts, we should live soberly, righteously, and godly, in this present world; *looking for that blessed hope, and the glorious appearing of the great God and our Saviour Jesus Christ.*" Titus 2:11-13.

235

"Looking forward to the happy fulfillment of our hopes when the splendor of our great God and Saviour Christ Jesus will appear," says the New English Bible.

That is just what the second advent is, and will be. While today it is our "blessed hope," when it actually occurs it will be the "happy fulfillment of our hopes." And not of ours only, but of all the people of God down the ages—millions upon millions of faithful Christians who, through the darkest times, have cherished the belief that someday the Lord will return in glory.

The apostle John was most definite on this matter: "Behold, He cometh with clouds," he wrote; "and every eye shall see Him." Revelation 1:7.

Later in the same book he describes the event itself, as he saw it in vision: "And I looked, and behold a white cloud, and upon the cloud One sat like unto the Son of man, having on His head a golden crown, and in His hand a sharp sickle. And another angel came out of the temple, crying with a loud voice to Him that sat on the cloud, Thrust in Thy sickle, and reap: for the time is come for Thee to reap; for the harvest of the earth is ripe." Revelation 14:14, 15.

Recording still another vision, he wrote: "I saw heaven wide open, and there before me was a white horse; and its rider's name was Faithful and True. . . . His eyes flamed like fire, and on His head were many diadems. Written upon Him was a name known to none but Himself, and He was robed in a garment drenched in blood. He was called the Word of God, and the armies of heaven followed Him on white horses, clothed in fine linen, clean and shining. From

His mouth there went a sharp sword with which to smite the nations; for He it is who shall rule them with an iron rod, and tread the winepress of the wrath and retribution of God the sovereign Lord. And on His robe and on His leg there was written the name: 'King of kings and Lord of lords.'" Revelation 19:11-16, N.E.B.

Why were the apostles so confident that Christ will return? Partly no doubt because of the Old Testament prophecies they knew so well, but chiefly because of Christ's own personal assurances. He left no doubt in anybody's mind as to the certainty of His second advent. He could not have been more explicit.

"Set your troubled hearts at rest," He said to them in one of His farewell messages. "Trust in God always; trust also in Me. There are many dwelling places in My Father's house; if it were not so I should have told you; for I am going there on purpose to prepare a place for you. And if I go and prepare a place for you, *I shall come again* and receive you to Myself, so that where I am you may be also." John 14:1-3, N.E.B.

At the time of His trial He said to Caiaphas, the high priest: "Hereafter shall ye see the Son of man sitting on the right hand of power, and coming in the clouds of heaven." Matthew 26:64.

At first it was not easy for the disciples to accept the idea that their beloved Master would leave them and defer His triumph to some distant day. They wanted Him to set up His kingdom there and then. Peter strongly resented the suggestion that He might be condemned to death and crucified. But gradually the truth dawned upon their minds that His return might be far in the future. This led them to ask Him, "Tell us, when shall these things be? and what shall be the sign of Thy coming, and of the end of the world?" Matthew 24:3.

This provided Jesus with an opportunity to clear up any misconception they might have had on this vital matter and to let them know how and when they might expect to see Him again. He took full advantage of it.

His greatest concern was lest they should be deceived by impostors.

"Take care that no one mislead you," He said. "For many will come claiming My name and saying, 'I am the Messiah;' and many will be misled by them." "If anyone says to you, 'Look, here is the Messiah,' or, 'There He is,' do not believe it. . . . If they tell you, 'He is there in the wilderness,' do not go out; or if they say, 'He is there in the inner room,' do not believe it. *Like lightning from the east, flashing as far as the west,* will be the coming of the Son of man." Matthew 24:4, 5, 23-27, N.E.B.

Turning to the matter of signs, He was equally forthright. They will, He assured them, be unmistakable.

One will be the proclamation of the gospel in all the world: "This gospel of the kingdom shall be preached in all the world for a witness unto all nations; and then shall the end come." Matthew 24:14.

Great calamities will have significance: "Nation shall rise against nation, and kingdom against kingdom: and great earthquakes shall be in divers places, and famines, and pestilences." Luke 21:10, 11.

Other signs will appear in the sky. "Fearful sights and great signs shall there be from heaven" (Luke 21:11), the sun being darkened, the moon becoming obscured, and great showers of meteors flashing through the atmosphere. Matthew 24:29.

Still other signs will appear in the councils of the nations and in the effect upon the masses of a disintegrating social order. "On earth nations will stand helpless, not knowing which way to turn from the roar and surge of the sea; men will faint with terror at the thought of all that is coming upon the world; for the celestial powers will be shaken. And then they will see the Son of man coming on a cloud with great power and glory." Luke 21:25-27, N.E.B.

How could Christ have spoken more clearly or made the truth about His second advent more plain? His will be no secret coming, to a desert place or a séance chamber. On the contrary, it will be as visible as the lightning and as audible as the thunder that follows it.

Nor will He come unannounced, without warning. Stupendous events both in the heavens and on the earth will herald the approach of that great day.

He left no loophole for doubt or misunderstanding. Thus His coming may rightly be numbered among the great certainties with which we may strengthen our hearts as we face the gathering storm.

There is a vital reason for doing so today, for the events of our time, and those now looming on the horizon, correspond exactly with those which Jesus said would be harbingers of His return.

Not only is the gospel being preached more widely

than ever, with the Bible now available in over 1,100 languages, but the darkening of the sun, the obscuring of the moon, and the falling of the stars are all in the past, amply fulfilled, as explained in detail in another volume.* Moreover, within the past half century the world has witnessed the greatest wars, famines, pestilences, and earthquakes since men first dwelt upon the earth. And one has but to consider the growing perils of the cold war, the ominous developments in Europe and Africa, the debacle in the United Nations, and the ever-present threat of nuclear destruction, to realize how extraordinarily applicable are the Master's words: "Nations will stand helpless, not knowing which way to turn."

The developing crisis is thus in very truth, as Daniel foretold, "the crisis at the close," marking the end of the age and declaring in trumpet tones that the coming of Christ is near, "even at the doors."

To some people this will not be good news. Indeed Jesus predicted that the vast majority will not be happy to see Him return. Said He: "Then shall all the tribes of the earth mourn." Matthew 24:30. It will mean too big an interruption of their selfish plans and worldly way of life.

When John beheld the second advent in vision he noted this lack of friendly welcome. Instead of being glad to see Him, "the kings of the earth, magnates and marshals, the rich and the powerful, and all men, slave or free, hid themselves in caves and mountain crags; and they called out to the mountains and the crags, 'Fall

*See *Your Bible and You,* pages 437-446.

on us and hide us from the face of the One who sits on the throne and from the vengeance of the Lamb.' For the great day of their vengeance has come, and who will be able to stand?" Revelation 6:15-17, N.E.B.

Not everybody, of course, will treat the returning Saviour thus. Isaiah tells how some will look up with gladness, crying, "Lo, this is our God; we have waited for Him, and He will save us: this is the Lord; we have waited for Him, we will be glad and rejoice in His salvation." Isaiah 25:9.

These will be God's faithful remnant, the people who have remained loyal and true to Him through all the trials and tribulations of the latter days. Looking upon them as He rides in glory down the skies, the Lord will recognize them as His own, saying, "Here are they that keep the commandments of God, and the faith of Jesus." Revelation 14:12. At that thrilling moment, with indescribable exultation, "He shall send His angels with a great sound of a trumpet, and they shall gather together His elect from the four winds, from one end of heaven to the other." Matthew 24:31.

Looking forward to this sublime climax of history we can see how many blessings it will bring. It will settle so many things that have needed settlement for a long, long time.

It will end the reign of sin. It will terminate all lawlessness. It will bring all despotisms down in ruin. As Paul wrote: "Then shall that wicked be revealed, whom the Lord shall consume with the spirit of His mouth, and shall destroy with the brightness of His coming." 2 Thessalonians 2:8.

At the same time it will be the beginning of a new and wonderful life for all who have loved the Lord in sincerity, both dead and living. Upon them will be conferred the priceless boon of immortality.

Suddenly, "in a moment, in the twinkling of an eye, at the last trump: . . . the dead shall be raised incorruptible, and we shall be changed. For this corruptible must put on incorruption, and this mortal must put on immortality. . . . Then shall be brought to pass the saying that is written, Death is swallowed up in victory." 1 Corinthians 15:52-54.

This will mean not only the end of death, but the end of all sickness and disease, the end of all pain and suffering, the end of every weakness and worry that have weighed upon the hearts of men. For immortality will bring with it perfect health, perennial well-being, the strength and vigor of eternal youth.

In that day "the eyes of the blind shall be opened, and the ears of the deaf unstopped; then shall the lame man leap like a hart, and the tongue of the dumb sing for joy." Isaiah 35:5, 6, R.S.V.

No wonder the prophet cried out in ecstasy: "Strengthen the weak hands, and make firm the feeble knees. Say to those who are of a fearful heart, 'Be strong, fear not! Behold, your God will come with vengeance, with the recompense of God. He will come and save you.'" Verses 3, 4, R.S.V.

He sensed what a mighty source of encouragement the contemplation of the second advent may be. The very thought of it, with all its innumerable blessings and the sheer joy of seeing Jesus face to face, will give strength to the weakest hands and keep the feeblest knees from shaking.

"Cast not away therefore your confidence, which hath great recompense of reward. For ye have need of patience, that, after ye have done the will of God, ye might receive the promise. For yet a little while, and He that shall come will come, and will not tarry." Hebrews 10:35-37.

With this wonderful certainty in our hearts we shall have all the courage we need to outlast the crisis and greet the Lord with joy.

17—C.F.C.

25

HEAVEN IS REAL

THANKS to the probing of space with rockets and satellites, old theories about heaven have been severely jolted. The long-held concept that the "saved" will float about on little white clouds strumming harps through all eternity has all but died out.

For this we should be thankful. Sitting on a cloud never appealed to me, let alone playing a harp forever and ever.

Heaven is not like that at all. Jesus did not die on Calvary to provide any such trivial and foolish future for those who accept His redeeming love and nobly follow His way of life. His plans call for something far different, something most wonderful and desirable, upon which all His wisdom and creative power have been bestowed.

As the apostle Paul wrote, "Eye hath not seen, nor ear heard, neither have entered into the heart of man, the things which God hath prepared for them that love Him." 1 Corinthians 2:9.

Misunderstandings concerning "heaven" result from a misuse of the word. Sometimes, quite properly, it is applied to the sky above us, as in the expression "the atmospheric heavens." Frequently it is thought of as referring to God's dwelling place where the "heavenly sanctuary" mentioned in the book of Hebrews is located, presumably at the center of His universe. See Job 22:12; 1 Kings 8:30.

Neither of these meanings has anything to do with the eternal home of the redeemed. This home will not be located far off in space, as we think of space today. It is going to be right here on the earth. It will be both real and practical, with nothing spooky or ethereal about it. Yet in truth it will be "heaven" because, besides being indescribably beautiful, it will also be the chosen dwelling place of Him who died to redeem it.

The Bible is most definite on this matter.

"The heaven, even the heavens, are the Lord's," wrote the psalmist, "but *the earth* hath He given to the children of men." Psalm 115:16.

"Evildoers shall be cut off: but those that wait upon the Lord, they shall inherit *the earth.*" Psalm 37:9.

"The righteous shall inherit *the land,* and dwell therein forever." Verse 29.

Jesus Himself declared, "Blessed are the meek: for they shall inherit *the earth*." Matthew 5:5.

Emphasis upon the earth as man's future home is very clear indeed. Of course, it will not be the earth in its present condition, bearing so many marks of sin. It will be the earth remade, transformed into the lovely place it was when first it came from the hands of the Creator.

The apostle Peter described this cleansing, renewing process in these words: "The day of the Lord will come as a thief in the night; in the which the heavens shall pass away with a great noise, and the elements shall melt with fervent heat, the earth also and the works that are therein shall be burned up. . . . Nevertheless we, according to His promise, look for new heavens and a new earth, wherein dwelleth righteousness." 2 Peter 3:10-13.

"On that day the heavens will disappear with a great rushing sound," says the New English Bible; "the elements will disintegrate in flames, and the earth with all that is in it will be laid bare. . . . But we have His promise, and look forward to new heavens and a new earth, the home of justice."

This is in complete harmony with the prophecy in the book of Isaiah: "Behold, I create new heavens and a new earth: and the former shall not be remembered, nor come into mind." Isaiah 65:17.

John likewise wrote in the book of Revelation: "I saw a new heaven and a new earth: for the first heaven and the first earth were passed away." Revelation 21:1.

There can be no question therefore that God's plan

is to re-create the present earth into a gloriously beautiful home for His people, where they will dwell in peace and happiness forever.

What about Paul's statement that the saints will be "caught up . . . to meet the Lord in the air" (1 Thessalonians 4:17), and Christ's promise that they will be taken to "many mansions" He has prepared for them? John 14:1-3.

There is no conflict. When Jesus returns in glory the saints *will* be caught up by angel hands to meet Him; they *will* follow Him in joyous procession to His Father's house. But they will go on a round-trip ticket. Revelation 20:4 suggests that they will stay there a thousand years, after which they will return to this earth for their permanent abode.

How very real this heavenly home will be is emphasized in Isaiah's prophecy concerning it. Speaking of its fortunate inhabitants he wrote: "They shall build houses, and inhabit them; and they shall plant vineyards, and eat the fruit of them. They shall not build, and another inhabit; they shall not plant, and another eat: for as the days of a tree are the days of My people, and Mine elect shall long enjoy the work of their hands." Isaiah 65:21, 22.

This does not mean that they will always be building houses and planting vineyards, but that they will employ their vigorous, creative minds in all sorts of worth-while activities

The marvelous beauty of this home will be equally real. Familiar sights may be missing, but new ones will be even more fascinating. There will be no vast deserts and oceans, for the whole globe will resemble Eden in all its primeval loveliness and charm. "The wilderness and the solitary place shall be glad for them; and the desert shall rejoice, and blossom as the rose. It shall blossom abundantly, and rejoice even with joy and singing: the glory of Lebanon shall be given unto it, the excellency of Carmel and Sharon, they shall see the glory of the Lord, and the excellency of our God." Isaiah 35:1, 2.

The peace of this home will be very real, too. No strife will interrupt it. There will be no wars, or struggles for supremacy, for there will be but one nation, one language, one King. "Then will I turn to the people a pure language, that they may all call upon the name of the Lord, to serve Him with one consent." Zephaniah 3:9.

There will be no lawlessness of any kind, for the commandments of God will be written upon every heart. Hebrews 8:10. Consequently no door will ever be locked and homes will have "neither bars nor gates." Ezekiel 38:11. Such protection would be superfluous, with the golden rule motivating every thought and deed of the entire populace.

Needless to say, the happiness of the people will also be real. Nobody will ever have to put on a smiling face to cover a heavy heart. There will be no heavy hearts. Families once broken by death, but reunited at the resurrection which takes place at Christ's second advent, will revel in joyous fellowship forevermore. "And God shall wipe away all tears from their eyes; and there shall be no more death, neither sorrow, nor crying, neither shall there be any more pain: for the former things are passed away." Revelation 21:4.

Gossiping tongues will never bring grief or worry to innocent people, for "the remnant of Israel shall not do iniquity, nor speak lies; neither shall a deceitful tongue be found in their mouth: for they shall feed and lie down, and none shall make them afraid." Zephaniah 3:13.

Everybody will be perennially healthy, which will be a reality of vital importance. "The inhabitant shall not say, I am sick." Isaiah 33:24. Nurses and doctors will have to turn their energies in other directions.

Nobody will ever be hungry, or in want, for the tree of life will be there bearing twelve kinds of fruit and yielding it "every month." Even its leaves will contain marvelous sustaining properties. Revelation 22:2.

The capital of this wonderful new earth will be the New Jerusalem, the very city Abraham saw in vision millenniums ago, "whose builder and maker is God." Hebrew 11:10.

There will be nothing insubstantial about this, although when John was shown it in vision he found it hard to describe. "It shone with the glory of God," he said. "It had the radiance of some priceless jewel, like a jasper, clear as crystal. It had a great high wall, with twelve gates, at which were twelve angels. . . . The wall was built of jasper, while the city itself was of pure gold, bright as clear glass. The foundations of the city wall were adorned with jewels of every kind. . . . The twelve gates were twelve pearls, each gate being made from a single pearl. The streets of the city were of pure gold, like translucent glass." Revelation 21:11-21, N.E.B.

Though overcome with the magnificence of the sight, he went on to record that he saw no temple there. Not a single church building! There will be no need for one, for the Lord Himself will be there. "And His servants shall serve Him: and they shall see His face." Revelation 22:3, 4.

This will be the supreme reality of this "heaven" on earth. For this intimate relationship between Christ and His redeemed will remain constant and unbroken through all eternity. As century succeeds century and age follows age, it will grow ever deeper, more sincere, more truly real.

Though He is King of kings and Lord of lords; though "His name shall be called Wonderful, Counselor, The mighty God, The everlasting Father, The Prince of Peace;" though "of the increase of His government and peace there shall be no end;" Jesus will ever be the gentle, loving Saviour to those He died to redeem. "For the Lamb which is in the midst of the throne shall feed them, and shall lead them unto living fountains of waters." Revelation 7:17.

A happy band of close-knit friends, they will roam the universe together, as the Master Teacher continues to unfold the mysteries of creation and inspire within them an ever-deepening insight into the wonders of God's love.

Such is the home that lies beyond the gathering storm. Though the choicest human words are totally inadequate to describe it, we may be sure that it will be the best that God can provide, completely and eternally satisfying.

This glorious "heaven" is no myth, no idle dream, no figment of the imagination. It will be as real as the creation we see about us today; a real home for real people. And it may be ours—yours and mine—if we want to share it.

Here is the divine invitation:

"The Spirit and the bride say, Come. And let him that heareth say, Come. And let him that is athirst come. And whosoever will, let him take the water of life *freely*." Revelation 22:17.

It is *all* free. The exquisite beauty. The wonderful peace. The abounding health. The magnificent city. The tree of life. The privilege of living forever with Jesus.

Here is a prize worth waiting for. Its dazzling light pierces the deepening gloom of these climactic years, bidding us keep up our courage and hold fast our faith.

With this great certainty to cheer us, the future holds no terrors we cannot face. Beyond the crisis lies the heaven of our dreams.

26

KEEP THE BELLS RINGING!

*H*ISTORY'S darkest periods have always produced men and women of vision and purpose to match the perils that faced them; and it will happen again today.

The stresses and trials of earth's final crisis will call forth people worthy of this mighty hour and ready to meet its challenge. Buttressed by faith and sustained by hope, they will stand resolute for God and the right whatever happens. Though the sword of Damocles fall, and the worst fears be realized, they will stand unmoved and immovable.

The years between A.D. 1450 and 1600 were marked by constant turmoil and bloodshed. Yet it was then that Bartholomeu Dias, in a tiny sailing vessel, rounded the Cape of Good Hope, Vasco de Gama found the sea route to India, and Balboa stood on a hill in Darien and saw the Pacific for the first time. Then it was that "there arose Columbus, the discoverer of a new world, Copernicus, the revealer of a new universe, and Luther, the forerunner of a new spiritual freedom."

From 1642 to 1649 civil war waged in England. Cavaliers and Roundheads battled for supremacy. The whole country was convulsed. Trade was at a standstill. Homes, castles, churches, cathedrals, were all involved in the mania for destruction. Yet at that very time someone, whose name has long since been forgotten, started to build a little country church, one of those lovely stone edifices which so enrich the English countryside with beauty.

Today on the wall of this church may be seen the following inscription:

"In the year 1643, when all things sacred were either demolished or profaned, this church was built by one whose singular praise it is to have done the best things in the worst times, and to have hoped them in the most calamitous."

In the same dark and perilous time John Milton wrote "Paradise Lost," while in 1665 and 1666—the very year of the great plague and fire of London— Isaac Newton, then but twenty-four years of age, made some of his most epochal scientific discoveries and wrote his famous law of gravity.

A hundred years later, on May 19, 1780, a great darkness suddenly covered all New England, so much so that thousands were terrified, sure that the Day of Judgment had arrived. But one man refused to be disturbed or deflected from his duty. John Greenleaf Whittier immortalized him in the poem "Abraham Davenport":

> 'Twas on a May day of the far old year
> Seventeen hundred eighty, that there fell
> Over the bloom and sweet life of the spring,
> Over the fresh earth and the heaven of noon,
> A horror of great darkness. . . .
> Men prayed, and women wept; all ears grew sharp
> To hear the doom-blast of the trumpet shatter
> The black sky. . . .
> Meanwhile in the old State House, dim as ghosts,
> Sat the lawgivers of Connecticut,
> Trembling beneath their legislative robes.
> "It is the Lord's Great Day! Let us adjourn,"
> Some said; and then, as if with one accord,
> All eyes were turned to Abraham Davenport.
> He rose, slow cleaving with his steady voice
> The intolerable hush. "This well may be
> The Day of Judgment which the world awaits;
> But be it so or not, I only know
> My present duty, and my Lord's command
> To occupy till He come. So at the post
> Where He hath set me in His providence,
> I choose, for one, to meet Him face to face,—
> No faithless servant frightened from my task,
> But ready when the Lord of the harvest calls;
> And therefore, with all reverence, I would say,
> Let God do His work, we will see to ours.
> Bring in the candles."

We need like Christian fortitude and devotion to duty today. Though the real day of judgment be upon